D1600231

A Sound Atlas of Irish English

Topics in English Linguistics
48

Editors

Bernd Kortmann
Elizabeth Closs Traugott

Mouton de Gruyter
Berlin · New York

A Sound Atlas
of Irish English

by

Raymond Hickey

Mouton de Gruyter
Berlin · New York

Mouton de Gruyter (formerly Mouton, The Hague)
is a Division of Walter de Gruyter GmbH & Co. KG, Berlin.

ISBN 3-11-018298-X

Bibliographic information published by Die Deutsche Bibliothek

Die Deutsche Bibliothek lists this publication in the Deutsche Nationalbibliografie;
detailed bibliographic data is available in the Internet at <http://dnb.ddb.de>.

Preface

This sound atlas offers a comprehensive audio overview of the English language as spoken in present-day Ireland. The data for the atlas was collected over several years during which the author travelled throughout the entire Republic of Ireland and Northern Ireland and collected anonymous samples of speech from representative speakers in both urban and rural settings and across at least three generations. The speakers in the samples are identified by gender, geographical location in Ireland and approximate age. The recordings were made on cassette tapes which were then digitised and compressed using the well-known MPEG Layer-3 method of sound file compression (often abbreviated to just 'MP3'). The material recorded for each speaker consisted of at least a list of sample sentences all of which illustrate the lexical sets (keywords illustrating the pronunciation of a sound) which are of interest in both northern and southern Irish English (see section II 5.1. *Lexical sets for Irish English* below). In many cases speakers also read a sample text which lasted approximately a minute and a half. This illustrates a more relaxed style as it is a continuous piece of text. Some speakers furthermore read a list of words which contained sounds critical for the present-day distribution of, and ongoing changes in Irish English. In all, there are over 1,500 recordings.

On the DVD accompanying this book all sound files are to be found as well as appropriate software for listening to the recordings. In addition there is much information about Irish English, an introduction to the phonology of this variety, as well as various items of background information which might be of interest to users of the atlas. Particular attention should be paid to the extracts of sound files in which many of the salient features of Irish English are discussed and illustrated. Together with the overview of Irish English, this offers an appropriate first orientation to the material on the DVD and to Irish English in general.

To install *A Sound Atlas of Irish English* on a PC you should run the setup programme to be found in the root directory of the DVD. The setup procedure is similar to that for any other programme running in a Windows environment. Users of the DVD should be aware that it requires approximately 3.2 GB (3,200 MB) of free space on your hard disk if you choose to install the sound files. However, if you choose not to copy the sound files to your hard disk, then only 160 MB are required.

You will then require the DVD to listen to the files. The programmes and the data can be removed completely if you wish to do so at some later date. To listen to the recordings you will require a functioning soundcard in your computer with speakers or headphones attached.

On the accompanying DVD there is also a so-called Java version of the sound atlas. Basically, this consists of software written in the programming language used for files in the internet. The great advantage here is that this programme will run under Windows and also on an Apple *Macintosh* computer (as well as under the Linux operating system and older versions of Windows). To start the Java version double click on the file 000_Sound_Atlas.htm (the first file in the root directory of the DVD) from within your file manager (on the desktop of the *Macintosh* or in the Windows *Explorer*). A programme will start showing a tree with options on the left of the screen and a window with information on the right corresponding to the currently active node. The opening screen shows a map of Ireland on the right with a list of the 32 counties. Choose a county from a list of sound files from speakers of that county and click on the ear symbol to listen to a recording. Users of the sound atlas should bear in mind that the Java version does not contain all the options present in the dedicated software written as a gateway to the atlas and which can be accessed by going through the setup procedure as described in the previous paragraph. But there are advantages to the Java version, not only that it is independent of computer type, as just mentioned, but also that it will run without installing any software or copying files from the supplied DVD to your computer.

At this point I would like to thank all the people in Ireland who provided me with a recording of their speech and without whose willing cooperation this project would not have been possible. Furthermore, I would like to express my gratitude to Essen University which generously funded the field trips for this atlas during the past few years. My thanks also go to Prof. Bernd Kortmann of the University of Freiburg for his willingness to accept this project for the series *Topics in English Linguistics* and last but not least I thank Dr. Anke Beck and Birgit Sievert of Mouton de Gruyter in Berlin for their encouragement and professional advice on publication matters.

Raymond Hickey
September 2004

Contents

I Data collection and analysis

1. Background to *A Sound Atlas of Irish English*

1.1. The beginnings with Dublin English

The sound files which represent the basis for *A Sound Atlas of Irish English* were collected over a period of several years, roughly from the mid 1990s to 2002. The sound atlas covers the whole of Ireland, i.e. all thirty two counties of the country. There has been a certain concentration on centres of population such as Dublin, Cork, Belfast or Derry but this has been dictated by numbers of speakers and not by any bias towards English at these locations.

      The beginnings of the current project lie in the investigations of Dublin English carried out by the present author starting in the late 1980s and early 1990s. From this the notion of a sound atlas evolved. The collection of data for such an atlas obviously requires a considerable degree of planning in advance. It also implies, by its very nature, that a few methods were tested until the final means of recording was chosen. This was indeed the case. For the earliest recordings a variant of the 'rapid and anonymous interview' as developed by Labov for his classical investigation of English in New York city (Labov 1996) was used. To begin with one must note that there are two types of anonymous interviews. The first is where the informant does not know that an interview is taking place. The second is where s/he does, but the name of the informant is not known to the investigator.

      The present author began with the first type of investigation. The object of the early recordings was the English of the capital Dublin. The reason for this is that the changes which Irish English has undergone in the past decade or so (Hickey 1999b) have emanated from Dublin to encompass the entire Republic of Ireland (but not Northern Ireland which is a different case). The initial investigations were concerned with changes which have been labelled the Dublin vowel shift (Hickey 1999b) and which basically concern the raising of the back vowels of the LOT, THOUGHT and NORTH lexical sets along with the onset of the diphthong in the CHOICE lexical set and possibly the retraction of the onset for the /ai/ diphthong (in words such as PRICE and PRIDE), though this last feature appears now (2004) to be recessive.

The purpose of the initial rapid anonymous interviews in the Dublin context was to obtain attestations for the /ai/ diphthong and in addition for the /ɔi/ diphthong. It was assumed that the onset of the latter diphthong would correlate with the position for the vowels of the LOT and THOUGHT lexical sets. These two sounds are labelled the (ai) and the (ɔi) variables respectively.

Locations of Dublin suburbs

A selection of locations in Dublin were chosen which were taken to be representative of both halves of the city. On the north side, two shopping centres were chosen in less residentially desirable areas: 1) the Northside Shopping Centre, close to the motorway and an industrial estate in Coolock and 2) the Omnipark Shopping Centre in Santry, near Ballymun, which contains Ireland's only group of high rise flats. These two locations were assumed (as it turned out, quite rightly) not to be areas in which would-be sophisticated urbanites would alter their speech to hive them off from the vernacular-speaking local population.

For the purposes of comparison two outlying shopping centres on the south side were also examined: 1) Stillorgan and 2) Cabinteely, both of which are several miles from the city centre as are the centres in Santry and Coolock (see overview map above).

The south side of the city begins on the south bank of the Liffey and for this reason the area around Grafton Street can be taken as representative of the south side commercially. The area around O'Connell Street is a transitional zone: it does not have the prestige of the southern bank of the Liffey but there are many specialist shops with a clear market niche, many established stores which date from before the post-war period when Dublin underwent considerable expansion. North of O'Connell Street a pattern is evident which is typical of modern suburb settlements, not just in Ireland: there are corner shops which provide for small needs, typically newsagents, tobacconists, grocery stores, often combined into one. Beyond that there are large shopping centres for one-stop shopping. These contain as their focus one or two large department stores with many smaller shops around them. Frequently the shops in such centres belong to chains of stores, found also in other shopping centres in other cities, apart from Dublin.

1.2. Conducting the interviews

For the interviews the author entered a particular shop and searched for an item on sale, preferably one which cost £5.99 (or later the equivalent in Euro currency) or indeed any price which ended in 99 pence/cent (practically all do and hence tags show this figure). Furthermore, he tried to ensure that the item was made in Ireland. He then approached the assistant and, feigning short-sightedness, asked what sum was on the price tag. Reading out the price provided a spontaneous pronunciation of the /ai/ diphthong before a voiced consonant, in *five* and in *nine* respectively. This is an environment in which the vowel shift, if present, was noticeable. The question was then repeated, which gave a more careful pronunciation of the same words.

Table 1. Structure of rapid anonymous interview, variant 1

Question 1:
> Hello, I'm afraid I don't have my glasses with me, could you tell me the price of this item?

Answer 1:
>   Five ninety nine [spontaneous style]

Question 2:
>   I beg your pardon?

Answer 2:
>   *Five ninety nine* [more careful style]

Now for the advance of the Dublin vowel shift, the pronunciation of the two key words *Ireland* and *Irish* was important. These words are obviously common and have high iconic value so that for many speakers the shift was particularly obvious in their realisation of the /ai/ vowel in these words. To elicit a pronunciation of these items, the following question was added to the above in each interview.

Table 2. Structure of rapid anonymous interview, variant 2

Question 3:
>   I wonder could you tell me where this item [garment, etc.] was made?

Answer 3:
>   In Ireland.

Question 4:
>   You mean it's not English?

Answer 4:
>   No, it's Irish.

The answers to questions 3 and 4 were not always predictable. The answers indicated above were given about half the time, but they varied from some other sentences like 'It's home-produced', 'It was made here alright' or just 'No' for question 4. This has meant that the amount of data here was much lower than for variant 1 of the interview.

   The pronunciation of the /ai/ vowel was recorded immediately after the brief interview. In this situation, the investigator had to remember the pronunciation as accurately as possible and for this reason only three variants were recognised although phonetically the range was much greater.

(1)   a.   /ai/   →   [əɪ]   (local)
       b.   /ai/   →   [aɪ]   (mainstream)
       c.   /ai/   →   [ɑɪ]   (fashionable)

The Dublin vowel shift would seem to be a push shift with the retraction of /ai/ providing the initial impetus for the change. This has meant that the /ɔi/ vowel which normally has a lowered and somewhat unrounded realisation in Irish English – [ɒɪ] – is realised close to [ɔɪ] in those varieties which have the vowel shift.

(2)		/ai/		/ɔi/
Local Dublin English		[əɪ]	–	[ɑɪ]
Mainstream Dublin English		[aɪ]	–	[ɒɪ]
Fashionable Dublin English		[ɑɪ]	–	[ɔɪ]

Testing for the (ɔi) variable within the present investigation was done in the following manner. The investigator ascertained whether the store in question had a department for children's toys and then engaged an assistant in the following brief exchange.

Table 3. Structure of rapid anonymous interview, variant 3

Question 1:
> I'm looking for something for my 8-year old nephew for his birthday, do you know where I might look?

Answer 1:
> Yeah, in the toy department. [spontaneous style]

Question 2:
> I beg your pardon?

Answer 2:
> Why don't you try the *toy* department. [more careful style]

The name of the department was offered in over 80% of cases. Sometimes an answer like 'In the kids'/children's department' was given which was not useful in the present context where the realisation of the (ɔi) variable was the object of interest. As with (ai), all realisations were assigned to one of three variants as follows.

(3) a.   /ɔi/   →   [ɑɪ]   (local)
     b.   /ɔi/   →   [ɒɪ]   (mainstream)
     c.   /ɔi/   →   [ɔɪ]   (fashionable)

An important result in this connection is that those speakers with the raised realisation of (ɔi) also had a retracted realisation of (ai) which would suggest that the former was caused by the retraction evident in the latter. It should be stressed that in the late 1990s and into the 2000s the retraction of /ai/ became recessive and is now regarded as a very dated feature. The raised realisations of /ɔi/ and the back vowels have, however, remained.

1.3. Results of the data collection

The method used for data collection in the initial Dublin survey turned out to be satisfactory. There were of course certain restrictions imposed by the method used. The most important was that the interviews were all very short and put a high demand on the memory of the investigator. The realisations which informants used had to be memorised and written down very soon afterwards, in effect the moment the investigator left the shop in question or merely moved away from an informant. The amount of data which can be recorded in this manner is quite limited but this is outweighed by the genuineness of the data and the certainty that informants are not influenced by prior knowledge of the investigation.

The data collected showed that an area in Dublin where the vowel shift was clearly represented was the up-market shopping area of Grafton Street and its neighbouring streets. A close examination in a number of selected shops was carried out after these initial results were obtained. To begin with the questions outlined above were posed, where appropriate. However, the results seemed to deliver an unexpected picture. The number of attestations of the vowel shift was not quite as high as expected, despite the previous uncoordinated observations made at these locations before the quantifying of data began in 1994.

The low ratings for the vowel shift which were obtained in the Grafton Street area could have been the result of the data collection method. However, there is no obvious reason why a method which worked in one part of the city should not do so in another part. Rather the ratings would seem to have the following cause. Retraction of (ai) arises from a relaxation of muscular tension for the onset of the diphthong. This is the articulatory directive for speakers wishing to distance themselves phonetically from the local [əɪ] realisation (Hickey 2000a). But during the anonymous interview, when presented with a question from a customer who claimed short-sightedness, a tenser and clearer articulation was used, even the first time round, which militated against the relaxation which is a precondition for (ai) retraction. That such a relaxation is the essential articulatory element with [ɑɪ] is supported by the fact that before voiceless consonants – which inherently involve a tenser articulation – the vowel shift is not attested.

In order to test the possible correctness of this analysis a further interview was designed and data was collected in 1996 and 1997. The area chosen was that of Grafton Street, a largely upmarket shopping area, just south of the centre of Dublin. In this case, only jewellery shops were chosen. The reason for this is that this type of shop caters for the better off section of society. However, the employees are usually young women who frequently come from a lower middle-class background. This is a scenario in which one finds the employees adapting their behaviour, linguistic and otherwise, to that of their clientele. This leads, of course, to hyperadaptation. Indeed it soon became obvious, that this group – young, lower middle-class females – was very active in the current vowel shift, if not in fact the prime motor in this development.

To ensure that a maximally relaxed interview could be conducted, a longer time was taken on each occasion. Furthermore, a time of day was chosen when the assistants were likely to be on their own, or with only one or two other customers in the shop. So the interviews were typically conducted early in the morning or during lunchtime, when business was slightly slacker. The verbal strategy employed was the following: the investigator entered the shop with the obvious intention of buying some jewellery. Approached by a shop assistant, he then asked for earrings with a Celtic design. This ensured that the word *design* occurred several times in the ensuing conversation. The phonotactic environment – /ai/ + voiced consonant – was that in which the vowel shift would be expected to manifest itself, if the interviewee had it. There was one slight disadvantage of this approach compared to the earlier type of interview based on feigned short-sightedness. Here the investigator had to place a request for a particular type of earring and hence may have, in one or two situations, provoked his type of pronunciation with assistants who showed a high degree of phonetic accommodation (Trudgill 1986). However, the use of the word *design* could be put to good use in this context. By employing a popular Dublin pronunciation – *design* [dəˈzəɪn] – the investigator was able to provoke the use of the shifted vowel – *design* [dəˈzɑɪn]. The reason for this lies in the motivation of the shift as a form of dissociation of the upwardly mobile group from local, working-class sections of the Dublin population (Hickey 2000a).

Table 4. Structure of longer anonymous interview

Introductory question:
      Hello, I'm looking for earrings for my wife. She's German and she'd like to have some with a Celtic design.
Typical initial response:
      Right, we've actually got quite a range with a Celtic design. Would you like to come over to the showcase and have a look . . .

After this opening a conversation of anything between 3 and 10 minutes ensued in which particular attention was paid to tokens of the /ai/ diphthong.

    The interpretation of the Dublin vowel shift as motivated by the desire for dissociation in language from the local population was once confirmed with particularly clarity during data collection when the investigator was in a Grafton Street jewellery shop early one morning. There was no-one in the shop apart from himself and a single shop assistant. After engaging in conversation on the matter of earrings for a few moments, he was presented with a few pairs which were prohibitively expensive. The assistant obviously noted the expression of surprise and dismay on his face and, as if to apologise for the pricing policy of her employers, immediately fell back into her native pronunciation, a clear local Dublin accent, and commented profusely on the cost of living and inflation in present-day Ireland. In this particular case it was plain that the young woman had adopted a new pronunciation which she felt was expected in her work environment, a pronunciation quite different from her own vernacular, that of lower-class north Dublin.

2. Recordings for *A Sound Atlas of Irish English*

In the late 1990s the author decided to expand the scope of the data recordings for Irish English beyond the capital Dublin. A much more comprehensive plan was evolved which was to encompass the entire island of Ireland. In addition the goal was not just to check for variable realisations which might or might not offer attestations of current changes in Dublin, although these were recorded as well. In terms of organisation, there is a clear contrast between the interviews from the early Dublin recordings and those for the later *Sound Atlas of Irish English* as can be seen from the following table.

Table 5. Organisation of interview for two main types of recording

	rapid	anonymous	unconscious
First Dublin recordings	x	x	x
Sound atlas recordings	–	x	–

By 'unconscious' here is meant that the informants are not aware that their language is being recorded, as in the classical 'rapid and anonymous interview' which originated with William Labov, see the methodological discussions in Labov (1966) .

The encounters for *A Sound Atlas of Irish English* were not interviews in a conventional sense of the word. They were recordings in which informants read either a list of short sentences, a stretch of text or perhaps a list of words (with some of the recordings done in Dublin), see sections 5.2. *Sample sentences*, 5.3. *Free text used for recordings* and 5.4. *Word list for critical pronunciations in Dublin English* below. There was no recorded verbal interaction, although some interaction did take place to convince people to participate in the recordings and often some discussion took place afterwards, typically with questions about what the purpose of the investigation was, what was going to happen to the data, what the results so far were like, etc. The amount of discussion varied greatly. In rural and small town settings with older individuals there was often considerable exchange with anecdotes involving experiences of the informants which had some relation to language and language use. Frequently the investigator was asked about the meaning of words or which of two possible expressions he thought the 'correct' one, going on the assumption that his profession as linguist gave him the right to pronounce on such matters.

2.1. Aim of the recordings

The goal of the sound atlas has been to provide a representative snapshot of contemporary Irish English with particular emphasis on the language of the younger generation. Because of the nature of data collection for such a large group of informants, the recordings were normally made in public. This meant that, despite later processing and filtering, background noise can be heard during many of the recordings. However, it is hoped that this is not intrusive. Users should be aware of the difficulties of obtaining good quality recordings in public places. It is only when one undertakes an enterprise such as the present one that one realises just how much ambient noise exists in modern urban surroundings. Some typical locations for recordings were on an open street (which accounts for some of the wind and traffic noise which can be heard on a few recordings) or in shopping malls and restaurants. The latter proved to be very favourable locations because people generally had a few minutes time and the public nature of the surroundings meant that they had no reservations in talking to the author. Again this type of location accounts for background noise such as the voices of others talking, people walking by, the clatter of plates and dishes, the movement of chairs and tables, etc. This noise was minimised by using a directional microphone and by later editing the recordings. Needless to say all recordings were anonymous.

Any investigation which purports to have produced an atlas for a variety must be comprehensive. The very title implies that there is full geographical coverage of Ireland. This also suggests that a large number of recordings are present in the sound atlas. An idea of the volume of the earlier and the later survey can be given by comparing numbers: the investigation of Dublin English in the mid 1990s resulted in some 140 recordings which were suitable for linguistic evaluation (Hickey 1999a). *A Sound Atlas of Irish English* on the other hand consists of over 1,500 recordings from nearly 1,200 speakers. Another major difference is that the earlier recordings for Dublin were not, given their nature, in audio format and hence were not digitised. In addition, the recordings for *A Sound Atlas of Irish English* were also rearranged as excerpts, providing individual lexical set realisations, for instance.

Table 6. Comparison of informants and recordings for two surveys

	no. of informants	no. of recordings
First Dublin recordings	*c* 140	*c* 140
Sound atlas recordings	1,194	1,517

2.1.1. Capturing variation

In the case of Irish English one is dealing with a collection of varieties. These are spoken across two countries which traditionally have had sets of varieties which show considerable differences between them (Barry 1981). Nonetheless there are island-wide characteristics which are not shared by varieties in Britain (Hickey 1999b) so that it appeared justified to cover the entire island of Ireland and treat all varieties found there within the framework of a single sound atlas.

In order to serve as a reference work, a sound atlas must encompass all sounds which might occur in any variety within the area considered and then register pronunciations of these in recordings. Designing a net to catch all sound features was the first task on the way to producing the sound atlas. The most unstructured method one could use would be to interview speakers and hope that in a sufficiently long stretch of speech everything would appear which was worth registering. There are three disadvantages to this, however. The first is that it requires the consent of informants to talk to the investigator for a length of time. Only a tiny minority were likely to engage in a conversation of this kind with a perfect stranger. The second disadvantage is that the amount of time required with this method is considerably greater than for the method which was actually used (see below). The third and obvious disadvantage is that one might still not obtain instances of all the sounds being investigated.

Given this situation, the choice fell for a method in which informants were presented with a set of short sentences, each of which contained a token of a particular lexical set, e.g. *He put his* FOOT *in it*. (the highlighting of keywords was not contained in the sentences presented to informants). In all 54 such sentences proved necessary. They fitted onto a single A4 page, an important factor as it is definitely off-putting if informants suspect that there is more to the investigation – timewise – than meets the eye, i.e. if there are several pages involved.

It should be mentioned that the words with which Wells (1982) chose to illustrate his lexical sets are frequently not very common. For instance, the lexical set which contains the /ʌ/ vowel is STRUT. However, the actual word *strut* does not occur anywhere in the informal recordings of Irish English which the present author has collected over the past decade or so, let alone occur in a form suitable for a digital recording. This means that the sound files which accompany the lexical sets contain pronunciations of some other word, e.g. *cut* for the STRUT lexical set (in the sample sentence *He* CUT *the piece of twine*). The same is true for the FLEECE lexical set. This was tested by using the word MEET in the sample sentence *They didn't bother to* MEET *him*.

2.2. Organisation of the recordings

The recording strategy which was then chosen involved informants reading a set of made-up sentences anonymously. Once speakers knew the investigation was anonymous, their readiness to participate rose dramatically. The anonymity was also important in order to process and later publish the recordings.

Certain types of organisation are automatically excluded if recordings are to be anonymous. It is not possible to do recordings in the interior of houses and keep them anonymous. So one of the scenarios considered during the planning phase – that of asking people in private 'bed and breakfast' houses – did not resonate with potential informants as was discovered during a short trial run and so the idea was abandoned.

The only solution was to do everything in the open – often on the street – as only there could one expect to meet potential informants in a completely anonymous context. However, there is one severe disadvantage with this scenario: streets are loud places and hence the quality of tape recordings is likely to suffer accordingly. Good equipment with a directional microphone is helpful, but the equipment must be physically small because large devices, such as a big microphone with a muffler, are intimidating. In fact the investigator held the small cassette recorder and the external microphone under the clipboard with the sample sentences so that it was not immediately obvious to those asked to participate that he wished to record them. It was only after saying that the recording was completely anonymous and consisted solely of made-up sentences that the cassette recorder was switched on and came into view. The external microphone improved the quality of the recordings and, importantly, allowed the investigator to stand back somewhat from the informant and so not intrude on his/her personal space, obviously a significant factor with younger female informants.

2.2.1. *Getting low noise recordings*

Users of *A Sound Atlas of Irish English* will notice that the recordings on the DVD mostly contain a relatively low level of background noise. This is due to a compromise between a purely outdoor and an indoor setting which was struck on for the recordings. When travelling around Ireland the author used a car rental and generally parked this right beside where he stood on the street addressing passers-by with a view to engaging them as informants. In some cases, particularly with males or older females, he asked them – after they had consented to do a recording – if they would mind stepping into the car as it was quieter. Generally, the informant consented, particularly as the car was parked with the passenger door facing onto the footpath and with the keys out of the ignition and lying in clear view on the dashboard in order to reassure the informant of the relative safety of stepping into the car. Where informants still had their doubts they were told they could of course leave the door open, this providing additional reassurance but leading to a deterioration of the recording depending on the traffic.

A few other public scenarios were used for recordings. Shopping malls proved a useful area to try and win informants. The corridors and staircases are open enough for people not to be apprehensive. However, here there is often noise from passers-by and the corridors of shopping malls tend to echo considerably. Schools and universities were used occasionally for pupils and students alike. In a few cases teachers were helpful and asked their pupils to cooperate. This was especially useful for recordings of Dublin English.

Lastly it should be mentioned that recordings were of course done out in the countryside. This locale provided an acoustic background of its own. Animals noises occasionally added some flavour to the background, but the major obstacle to contend with was wind. Fortunately, various options of the digitisation software made it possible to filter out the noise of the wind to a large extent, but it can still be heard as a background rumble on many recordings.

3. Analysing the recording exchanges

The types of exchange which occur when compiling a sound atlas are not like normal conversation. They are not two way exchanges (except for the initiating and concluding phase which are not part of the recording and which were not taped – this fact was obvious to informants). Recordings do not involve backchannelling, there are no supportive noises during the contact. In fact the taped recording is an exercise in reading text aloud. Occasionally, if informants were having difficulty or asked something about the sample sentences, a brief exchange occurred. This was then cut out during editing for later digitisation.

The following remarks are thus about the exchanges surrounding the recording. The concluding phase is not really important as it just winds up the exchange. A few brief remarks, an expression of thanks and a wish for a pleasant day, were all that occurred here.

The most interesting part was obviously the initiating phase. This was about convincing a stranger to offer a brief service, that of reading a set of sentences out loud and permitting the investigator to tape them. It involved two participants, the investigator and the informant with the goal of recording the informant. But in a number of cases, there was more than one informant. If two people (rarely more) were addressed then the first choice to be made was who to focus on and persuade to do the recording. In fact certain techniques worked fairly well in small groups, three or more. For instance, the use of flattery, if only jocularly, was only a last resort with an individual, but usually worked well with a group. Fixing on one member of the group and making a not-too-serious remark like 'You look like a natural leader' often worked and the individual was bolstered by this flattery in front of others into participating.

3.1. Minimising social distance for recordings

A feature of Irish social interaction is that it tends to require the participants to show little social distance, and if it is obvious that this exists, it should not be highlighted or foregrounded in conversation. In this respect many exchanges are different from those in other countries, for example in Germany.

Paying attention to this feature is important in linguistic surveys and the investigator was careful not to highlight the fact that he was an academic. One convenient means of minimising social distance was to emphasise the fact that the author was employed by a university department to carry out the investigation, and that the survey was not his own idea.

In the initial phase of data collection the author identified himself clearly as the originator of the investigation. The strategy here was to be maximally honest in the expectation that this would provoke cooperation on the part of potential informants. However, this did not produce the desired effect and the author quickly abandoned it for a position where he maintained that he was an employee of a university and that he was working for a professor there.

3.2. Effort and intrusion

When trying to persuade people to participate in a survey there are two aspects which one should try to keep to a minimum and, if at all, just remark on their slight nature. The first could be dubbed 'The principle of minimal effort' and is foregrounded by pointing out the small number of sentences. In this respect the rather vague time references used by the Irish are helpful. A typical remark by the investigator was 'It only takes a minute' or even 'It only takes a sec'. The latter is obviously meant metaphorically but the reference to a minute was not quite accurate either. The average reading time for the 54 sample sentences was between one and a half and two minutes.

The second aspect which should be highlighted might be labelled the 'The principle of minimal intrusion'. By that is meant that the investigator is aware of the imposition on the potential informant which his request implies and is apologetic about this. This can be done by remarks such as 'I don't want to bother you know, but perhaps you have a few secs'.

3.3. Asking permission

One feature of the unconscious interview is that the investigator does not have to ask permission (Grundy 1995: 161-4). For the sound atlas recordings this was, however, necessary. This simple fact introduced an added dimension to the recordings which involved careful planning by the investigator and in many cases considerable persuasion to convince people to participate.

Authors who have concerned themselves with linguistic surveys (Stubbs 1983: 17) identify several components of the approach made to a potential informant, e.g. (1) opener + (2) identification + (3) explanation.

1) *Opener* This is the very beginning of the exchange. When soliciting recordings from potential informants, the opener had the form of an apology for disturbing someone (see previous section) followed by a request, i.e. something along the lines of the following: 'Sorry to bother you, but I wonder if you'd have a moment?' or 'Excuse me, could I speak to you for a moment?'

A peculiar aspect of openers in the present context is that they had to be very short. One must bear in mind that the investigator was usually standing on the street and potential informants were walking by. When addressed by the investigator, most people did not stop but merely slowed down, so that the opener had to be brief, otherwise people would already be out of earshot before it was finished.

Another feature of openers is that they should never offer a potential informant an easy chance to say 'no'. It would be disastrous to use an opener like 'I'm sure you're very busy, but ... ' because all the informant has to do is to say 'Yes I am' and walk away.

An opener may often contain an element of justification for what one is doing. Most people in present-day Ireland assume that someone who addresses them on the street with a clipboard in his/her hand and an identification badge around his/her neck is there for a commercial reason. To counter this suspicion the investigator often followed the opener by saying very quickly: 'I am not trying to sell anything'. This had the advantage of stopping people who were curious about the purpose of the apparent survey. Another remark – 'I am not a religious sect' – dispelled a further suspicion which may have arisen. After this, the curiosity of passers-by often caused them to stop and turn to the investigator. This led to the next component of the exchange.

2) *Identification* Whether it is important for potential informants to know the investigator's name is not certain. However, offering identification immediately does seem to convey a sense of everything being open and above board and hence offers reassurance to potential informants. Identification by just saying the following sentence, possibly with the information in brackets also, was generally sufficient: 'My name is Ray Hickey (from UCD in Dublin)'.

3) *Explanation* A brief non-technical account of what the survey was about gave the best chance of obtaining a recording. Something like 'We're doing a survey of English spoken in present-day Ireland' (note the use of the plural pronoun which had a reassuring effect on many). For some people this simple explanation was enough. For others more information was appropriate. In some instances it helped to show the relevance to other aspects of contemporary life. Comments like the following were then offered: 'Well, you know the way things are changing so fast and we were just wondering if this also applies to the way people talk as well'. The kind of detail offered varied depending on the particular location. Outside of the capital in the Republic of Ireland one could refer to changes in Dublin and mention that one is interested in seeing if these are spreading to the rest of the country. Here the 'righteous indignation' factor came into play as people outside of Dublin generally deplored what they regarded as conceited accents from the capital.

3.4. Appeals for participant help

If potential informants were reluctant to cooperate then the investigator pointed out that he was only doing this job to keep body and soul together and that the informants could help him by participating. This could be augmented by additional remarks like: 'It would be a great help. My boss would be pleased if I could get a number of people from this area'. Such appeals were based on a putative 'feel good' factor which informants experienced if they decided to help.

On occasions the investigator remarked – briefly and positively – on the speech of an individual. However, it was necessary to be careful here. It was not advisable to focus too much on the accent of the informants as this tended to make them self-conscious, something which could have backfired when requesting participation. However, this approach was used in moderation and was often successful in convincing reluctant informants to participate.

As a last resort downright flattery was tried. Comments such as 'You have a lovely clear accent', 'You speak very distinctly', 'You have good delivery' were tried on occasion. The disadvantage here is that this only works – if at all – with middle class, non-local speakers. There is no point in praising the accent of a local Dubliner, for instance. Understandably, the individual is liable to feel that s/he is being made fun of.

3.5. Righteous indignation and survey fatigue

It is a well-known ploy in sociolinguistic investigations to broach a subject matter which induces a sense of righteous indignation in potential participants. For example, given the Irish context of the survey, it was often beneficial to remark (in a more lengthy opening exchange) about the cost of living, the level of taxes, the corruption of politicians or whatever.

On occasions it was also useful to pre-empt objections by possible informants. Now and then the investigator chose to explicitly mention 'survey fatigue' which one may expect informants to suffer from. This was indeed the case in Belfast and Derry which, because of the violent disturbances during the 'Troubles' (the three decades up to the mid 1990s), have been the scenes of many sociological surveys. By deliberately addressing this issue, it was possible to take the wind out of people's sails so to speak and achieve their participation after all.

3.6. Face of the informants

While it is true that the actual tape-recording of informants was not a two-way exchange as found in normal conversation, a certain amount of backchannelling was required with some informants to make them feel more relaxed. If someone faltered during the sentences – and this often happened with older rural speakers – then support was offered by saying something like 'You're doing fine', 'That's grand', 'Lovely, no problem now' which usually put them at their ease.

If at the very beginning a potential informant refuses flatly to perform a recording, there is nothing one can do. Irish people do not usually revise a decision they make, especially for a stranger. This situation is in contrast to that in, say, Germany where one can offer cogent reasons for participation and perhaps win an individual over to one's point of view.

The upshot of this is that one should always immediately accept 'no' as an answer in an Irish context. There is another important reason for not pushing the matter: many people in Ireland, certainly older rural inhabitants, are not able to read. This accounts for many friendly encounters where people nonetheless declined, saying something like 'Ah no, you're fine now. Thanks very much' or 'No, listen, thanks very much now. I'm sure you'll find plenty of other people'.

Some excuses for not cooperating were offered simply because the potential informants were not interested. Questions were asked like 'Will you be here tomorrow?'. Or someone passing in a certain direction would say 'I'll catch you on the way back'. Some individuals even claimed 'I've done that already' in a locality where the investigator had never been before in his life.

4. Background to *A Survey of Irish English Usage*

The following paragraphs describe the collection done for *A Survey of Irish English Usage*, a parallel survey undertaken by the author during recordings for *A Sound Atlas of Irish English*. As the work involved a different medium (a questionnaire) and different participation by members of the public (just ticking boxes after sentences) it is interesting to compare this work to that for the sound atlas.

To the pleasant surprise of the investigator the readiness to participate by filling in a questionnaire was virtually universal throughout all
counties of Ireland. The idea of doing a questionnaire seemed to arouse
people's interest. As questionnaires in surveys are nearly always anonymous, there was no need to highlight this aspect, it was taken for
granted. The fact that participants did not have to speak probably added
to their almost automatic readiness to take part.

Although no persuasion was necessary, there are nonetheless a
few factors which are important when carrying out such a survey. The
first rule – which the investigator can confirm after his experience – is:
'Never do questionnaires with single individuals'. Their behaviour
immediately becomes prescriptive and they start rejecting structures
which they would probably use themselves. Instead one should work
with small groups. As the acoustic factors, such as background noise or
wind, which were critical with the sound atlas recordings, were
irrelevant here, the groups could be anywhere, in a loud pub, a noisy
restaurant, even in the waiting hall of the central bus station in Dublin.
The clue to minimising the chance of rejection was to begin passing a
potential participant a questionnaire while still asking if s/he wished to
take part. People usually react to being passed something by reaching out
to take it and once they had the questionnaire in their hands they were
unlikely to hand it back and decline to participate.

Avoiding prescriptivism is a matter which requires attention
during a survey of this nature. At the top of the questionnaire the
question was asked 'How do you find the following sentences (in casual
speech among your friends)?'. This was mentioned again when
participants began to look at the questionnaire. The investigator tried to
convey a casual attitude to the task and, for instance, never said that he
was from a university department, unless asked and then only after the
questionnaire had been filled in.

Working in groups has the advantage that the members are more
relaxed than individuals. The focus is then not concentrated on the
investigator and a single participant but rather on the group in which
there was usually considerable rapport as the members tended to be
friends anyway. They frequently read the sentences out loud to each
other and compared notes (the investigator always stood some distance
away from the group while they were filling in the questionnaire). If
someone complained that a certain structure, such as 'What are youse up

to?' was unacceptable, someone else often said something like 'What? You just said it to us a moment ago!'.

The attention span for a questionnaire is usually two to three minutes. The 57 sentences of the questionnaire could be ticked within this time. However, participants all showed a fall off in attention towards the end, so that structures which were not so important were included on the last page of the questionnaire. Furthermore, it is essential in a questionnaire survey that participants answer the question in a genuine manner. Thus any questionnaires in which most structures were accepted or rejected were discarded. There had to be at least a 10% fluctuation in acceptance. Otherwise it was obvious that the participant did not take sufficient care with the task. This condition meant that, of some 1,300 questionnaires which were returned, just over 1,000 were used for the survey and converted into database form for later processing via the dedicated software written by the author (see IV *A Survey of Irish English Usage* below).

Finally it should be mentioned that the awareness of grammatical structures varied greatly among participants. Many of them asked the investigator what was 'strange' or 'wrong' or 'particularly Irish' about a certain structure. This showed that speakers perception of non-standard structures in their variety of English varied considerably. For instance, many participants in the survey saw nothing strange in (1) *I know her for five years now* (extended present) or (2) *She has the housework done* (resultative perfect with OV word order) or (3) *They're finished the work now* ('be' as an auxiliary). On the other hand other structures were obviously very salient for speakers, such as (1) *I seen him yesterday* (past participle as preterite) or (2) *Them shoes are too small for me* (*them* as demonstrative pronoun).

II The English language in Ireland

1. Introduction

The following sections offer an overview of the development and present-day forms of the English language in Ireland. The purpose of including this here is to provide the users of the sound atlas with a concise summary of the basic facts concerning different forms and stages of Irish English. More detailed comment and analysis are to be found in Hickey (2004) – for phonology – and in Filppula (1999, 2004) – for morphology and syntax. Furthermore, readers interested in pursuing matters relevant to Irish English should consult the many references in the source book for Irish English published as Hickey (2002).

1.1. Dialect divisions

There are thirty two counties in present-day Ireland distributed in somewhat uneven fashion across four provinces. The counties vary in size, Cork and Galway being the largest, Louth and Carlow the smallest. The population of counties depends on whether they contain large towns or cities. Some counties, like Leitrim and Clare, do not have an associated town or city, while other do, e.g. Limerick, Cork, Wexford, etc.

The province of Ulster contains nine counties, six of which are within the borders of Northern Ireland, the small state formed on the partition of Ireland in 1921. There is a limited presence of Ulster Scots speech outside of Northern Ireland, in the Lagan district of north-west Donegal. Features of northern speech, especially the fronted [ʉ] sound in the GOOSE lexical set, spread much further southwards than previously thought and are attested in the recordings of the sound atlas.

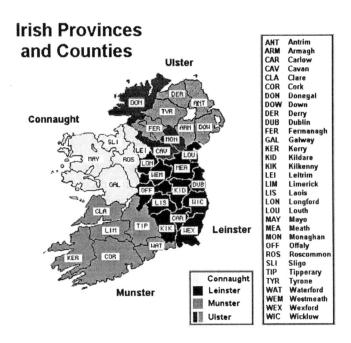

Irish Provinces and Counties

ANT	Antrim
ARM	Armagh
CAR	Carlow
CAV	Cavan
CLA	Clare
COR	Cork
DON	Donegal
DOW	Down
DER	Derry
DUB	Dublin
FER	Fermanagh
GAL	Galway
KER	Kerry
KID	Kildare
KIK	Kilkenny
LEI	Leitrim
LIM	Limerick
LIS	Laois
LON	Longford
LOU	Louth
MAY	Mayo
MEA	Meath
MON	Monaghan
OFF	Offaly
ROS	Roscommon
SLI	Sligo
TIP	Tipperary
TYR	Tyrone
WAT	Waterford
WEM	Westmeath
WEX	Wexford
WIC	Wicklow

The south of Ireland can be divided into two broad dialect regions. The first and oldest is the east coast dialect area which stretches from Waterford up to beyond Dublin, probably to Dundalk and beyond in its original extension before 1600.

The second area is that of the south-west and west and is the part of the country which was latest to engage in the language shift from Irish to English. Indeed for a few small pockets on the western seaboard, in Kerry, Connemara and Donegal, the Irish language has not died out yet.

In the centre and north-central part of the country there is a diffuse and dialectally indeterminate Midlands region which extends from southern Offaly and Laois up to Cavan and south Leitrim.

Between Sligo in the west and Dundalk in the east there is a broad transitional band which shows a mixture of southern and northern features (see discussions below).

areas with largest
Irish-speaking
populations

Ulster Scots

brought by
17c planters

Mid-Ulster
English

Donegal

Derry

Belfast

Sligo

Dundalk

Westport

Midlands

Dublin

Connemara

Galway

East Coast
Dialect Area

area of original
settlement in
late 12c by
Anglo-Normans

Limerick

Kerry

Tralee

Waterford

Cork

Forth
and Bargy

archaic dialect,
died out early 19c

South-West
and West

The north of Ireland consists of the counties of Ulster and can be divided into a large central region, that of Mid-Ulster English, and a 'Coastal Crescent' (Gregg 1972, 1985) running from Co. Down, south-east of Belfast, up to Antrim in the extreme north-east, through Co. Derry and across to the north-east of Donegal (but excluding the city of Derry). This area is that of strongest Scottish settlement and hence it represents Ulster Scots in its most original form (there are also some other smaller areas, such as north Co. Armagh, see Corrigan 1999). In the west of Donegal, forms of Ulster English in contact with Irish are spoken (see the partial study by Ní Chasaide 1979).

1.2. Historical background

The most cursory glance at the history of Irish English reveals that it is divided into two periods. The first period starts in the late 12th century with the arrival of the first English-speaking settlers and finishes around 1600 when the second period opens. The main event which justifies this periodisation is the renewed and vigorous planting of English in Ireland at the beginning of the 17th century. During the first period the Old English – as this group is called in the Irish context – came increasingly under the influence of the Irish. The Anglo-Normans who were the military leaders of the initial settlement had been completely absorbed by the Irish by the end of the 15th century. The progressive Gaelicisation led the English to attempt planting the Irish countryside in order to reinforce the English presence there. This was by and large a failure and it was only with James I that successful planting of (Lowland Scots and English) settlers in the north of the country tipped the linguistic balance in favour of English in the north. During the seventeenth century (after the Cromwellian campaigns at the middle of the century) new forms of English were brought to Ireland, Scots in the north and West/North Midland varieties in the south (where there had been a predominantly West Midland and South-West input in the first period). Although there was renewed Anglicisation, there is a definite continuation of south-west English features, which stem from the imported varieties of the first period, on the east coast, in Dublin and other locations down to Waterford in the south-east. This fact underlies a distinctive east coast dialect area (see comments above).

1.3. The medieval period

The documentary record of medieval Irish English is confined for all intents and purposes to the collection of 16 poems of Irish provenance in BM Harley 913 which are known collectively as the *Kildare Poems* (Heuser 1904, Lucas 1995) after one of the poems in which the author identifies himself as from the county of Kildare (to the south-west of Dublin). The collection probably dates from the early 14th century. The language of these poems is of a general west Midland to southern English character. Many of the idiosyncratic features can be traced to Irish influence (see discussion in Hickey 1993). It is a moot point whether the *Kildare Poems* were written by native speakers of Irish using English as a H-language in a diglossic situation and whether indeed the set was written by one or more individuals. Apart from the *Kildare Poems* medieval Irish English is attested in a number of verse fragments and in city records from Dublin and Waterford, comments on which can be found in Henry (1958) and Hickey (2001).

1.4. The early and late modern period

At the end of the 16th century attestations of Irish English begin to appear which are deliberate representations of the variety of the time. These are frequently in the guise of literary parody of the Irish by English authors (see the discussions in Bliss 1976, 1979; Sullivan 1976, 1980). The value of these written representations of Irish English for reconstructing the language of the time has been much questioned and it is true that little if any detail can be extracted from these sources. In addition most of the satirical pieces were written by Englishmen so that one is dealing with an external perception of Irish English at the time. Satirical writings are not the only source of Irish English, however. There are some writers, especially in the 19th century, who seriously attempt to indicate colloquial speech of their time, such as Maria Edgeworth in her novel *Castle Rackrent* (1801).

1.5. Language shift in early modern Ireland

Literary parodies do not reveal anything about the then relationship of Irish to English, the spread of English and the regional input from England. There were no censuses before 1851 which gave data on language use. Adams (1965) is a useful attempt to nonetheless produce a linguistic cartography of Ireland at the beginning of the early modern period. The upshot of this situation is that there is no reliable data on the language shift which began in earnest in the early 17th century and which had been all but completed by the late 19th century.

It is clear that the Irish learned English from other Irish who already had some knowledge of the language, perhaps through contact with those urban Irish who were English speakers, especially on the east coast and through contact with the English planters and their employees. This fact had consequences for the nature of Irish English. Bliss (1977) maintained that this fact was responsible for both the common malapropisms and the unconventional word stress found in Irish English. However, the stress pattern in verbs with final long vowels, e.g.

distribute [dɪstrɪˈbjuːt], *educate* [ɛdjuˈkeːt], can also be due to English input, particularly as the late stress (used by Bliss as an argument) is only a feature of southern Irish, not of the west and north, and so influence due to contact with Irish could only be posited for the south of Ireland.

1.6. Contact Irish English

In present-day Ireland there are only a few small remaining enclaves scattered along the western seaboard where Irish is still spoken as a native language in a situation of unbroken historical continuity. In principle this setting should be the one in which the language shift scenario of previous centuries (Hickey 1995) is replicated, thus enabling linguists to view the process of language contact and transfer *in vivo*. Despite this fact there are few studies of contact Irish English today although the Irish language in contact areas has repeatedly being the subject of investigation, e.g. Stenson (1991). One notable exception to this is Ní Chasaide (1979). This study was carried out on seven informants from the north west of Ireland (Co. Donegal) to see what kind of /l/ sounds they showed in English. To this end their Irish was investigated. This variety of Irish shows three types of *l*-sound: a velarised [ɫ], a palatalised [ʎ] and a (lenited) neutral [l]. It turned out that the speakers used the last sound as the realisation of English /l/ in all positions (bar before /j/ as in *million* /mɪljən/ = [mɪʎən]) which tallies with the realisation of /l/ in the rest of the country where this was decided a century or two ago.

1.7. Supraregionalisation

It is obvious from English loanwords in Irish that early Irish English had not progressed through the major long vowel shift in England, e.g. Irish *bacús* 'bakehouse' shows unshifted /aː/ and /uː/. The play *Captain Thomas Stukeley* (1596/1605), the first widespread representation of Irish English in literary parody (Bliss 1979), consistently uses <*oo*> for words with /au/ from Middle English /uː/, e.g. *toon* for *town*. Furthermore, comments from Thomas Sheridan in the late 18th century (Sheridan 1781) show that Middle English /aː/, as in *patron,* still had not shifted, nor had Middle English /ɛː/ as in *meat*. But present-day Irish English shows little or no trace of these unshifted vowels (none of unshifted /uː/). The reason is not that the shift took place in Irish English some time in the 19th century but that the unshifted forms were replaced by mainstream English pronunciations due to a process called *supraregionalisation* (Hickey 2003c). The essence of this process is the replacement of salient features of a variety (Hickey 2000b) by more standard ones, frequently from an extranational norm, as with southern British English vis à vis Irish English. The motivation for this move is to render a variety less locally bound, more acceptable to a non-vernacular community, hence the term *supraregionalisation*.

1.8. Vernacularisation

The story of supraregionalisation does not end with the disappearance of strongly local features. There is another pathway which such features can take. This is the relegation to vernacular varieties. Take the instance of Middle English /ɛː/ as in *beat* /bɛːt/. This pronunciation is now confined to strongly local varieties where supraregionalisation has not taken place. Furthermore, non-local speakers can style-shift downwards to achieve a vernacular effect. Another example of this would be the use of *youse* or *yez* for the second person plural. This is shunned by non-local speakers but can be employed when deliberately switching to a vernacular mode.

The process of vernacularisation has in some instances led to a lexical split. Consider the reflex of velariscd [ɫ] before [d] in Irish English: this is the diphthong [au] as in the words *old* [aul] and *bold* [baul] with the post-sonorant stop deletion common in local forms of Irish English. These forms are available alongside /oːld/ and /boːld/ to non-local speakers but the meanings are somewhat different as the original forms with [au] have gained additional meaning components: [aul] 'old + affectionate attachment', e.g. *His* [aul] *car has finally given up the ghost*, [baul] 'daring + sneaking admiration', e.g. *The* [baul] *Charlie is back on top again.*

2. Varieties of Southern Irish English

It is obvious that linguistically, as well as politically, Ireland is divided into two broad sections, the north and the south. The former consists of the six counties presently within the state of Northern Ireland and of the large county of Donegal which is part of the Republic of Ireland. The north has a complex linguistic landscape of its own with at least two major historical varieties, Ulster Scots, the speech of those directly derived from the original Lowland Scots settlers, and Mid-Ulster English, the speech of those descendants of English settlers to central parts of Ulster. In addition there is the sociolinguistically complex capital, Belfast. Co. Donegal by and large goes with the rest of Ulster in sharing key features of English in the province and also in the varieties of Irish used there.

The north of the country is quite distinct from the south, accents of northerners being immediately recognisable to southerners. A dividing line can be drawn roughly between Sligo, just south of Co. Donegal to Dundalk on the east coast immediately below the border with Northern Ireland (Ó Baoill 1991, Barry 1981). North of this line the accents are distinctly Ulster-like. South of this line the northern features rapidly give way to southern values. The term 'line' here might imply a clearly delimited boundary, perhaps 'zone' might be more accurate as border counties such as Monaghan, Cavan or Louth show mixed accents which have adopted features from both northern and southern types.

The transition can be seen clearly moving down the east coast: Dundalk has a northern flavour to its speech but this is more of less lost by the time one reaches Drogheda travelling southwards. However, the recordings of *A Sound Atlas of Irish English* show that key features of northern Irish English, such as mid front vowel breaking, as in *save* [seəv], and *u*-fronting, as in *boot* [bʉt], extend quite far down the east coast, indeed in the case of the latter almost to the border of Co. Dublin.

Northern features which occur in the transition zone from south to north
Use of ambidental fricatives for dental stops in the south
Use of a fronted allophone of /uː/ and /u/, i.e. [ʉ]

A reduction in the vowel length distinctions
Use of a retroflex [ɹ] in syllable-final position
Greater pitch range between stressed and unstressed syllables
Greater allophony of /æ/, e.g. raised variants in a velar environment *bag* [bɛg] and a retracted realisation in a nasal environment *family* ['fɑmli]
Recessive occurrence of glides after velars and before front vowels as in *Cavan* ['kjævən] (a border county)

2.1. The East Coast

The east of the country stretches from the town of Dundalk north of Dublin down to Waterford in the south-east and includes such towns as Carlow, Kilkenny, New Ross, Wexford. This is the area which was first settled by the English from the late 12th century onwards and it is roughly coterminous with that which was encompassed by the Pale, the region of English influence in the late medieval ages, at its greatest extension (Dudley Edwards 1981 [1973]: 91). The original input from South-West England did in fact survive in altered form until the beginning of the 19th century in the archaic dialect of Forth and Bargy which was recorded by a few glossary compilers before it finally ceased to exist (Hickey 1988).

East band features from Dundalk down to Waterford (including Dublin)
Fortition of dental fricatives to alveolar stops (also south), e.g. *think* [tɪŋk]
Lack of low vowel lengthening before voiceless fricatives (not Dublin), e.g. *path* [pat]
Front onset of /au/, e.g. *town* [tæʊn], [tɛʊn]
Centralised onset of /ai/ (also south), e.g. *quite* [kwəɪt]
Breaking of long high vowels (especially Dublin), e.g. *clean* [klɪʲən]
Fortition of alveolar sibilants in pre-nasal position (especially south-east), e.g. *isnt* [ɪdn̩t]

No lowering of early modern /u/ (only Dublin), e.g. *done* [dʊn]
Glottalisation of lenited /t/ (especially Dublin), e.g. *foot* [fʊt] → [fʊt̞] → [fʊʔ] → [fʊh].

2.2. The South-West and West

This is a large region, from Co. Cork up to Co. Mayo, and was that in which Irish survived longest (Hindley 1990). As rule of thumb one can say that Irish receded from east to west (Ó Cuív 1969). Furthermore, in this western and southern half of the country there is no survival of English from the first period with the possible exception of very small pockets in the major cities Cork, Limerick and Galway. Hence the English which developed here was that of the early modern period which arose through uncontrolled adult second language acquisition on the part of the rural inhabitants who represented the vast majority of speakers. Furthermore, the regional English input of the early modern period was of a largely West Midlands character.

The south-west and the west can also be distinguished from each other, at least on phonological grounds. The major segmental feature is the raising of /ɛ/ → /ɪ/ before nasals in the southwest. However, it is not a decisive feature in separating these areas as this raising is found up as far as south Galway. In this respect nasal raising can be compared to *u*-fronting in the north (see section 3.4. *Contrasting northern and southern Irish English* below). U-fronting is definitely a characteristic of northern speech but it is found quite far down in the south, at least down into Co. Meath. To say it is found there does not make it a feature of general speech in that region. Rather one can state that it is a conservative feature which extends quite far south but is not part of supraregional speech there, but it is in the north of Ireland.

Nasal raising is similar in the south-west and west. In the former area it is widespread and found across different speaker groups. In the lower west (Clare, south Galway) it is also found, but it is restricted to conservative vernacular varieties as opposed to areas further south – in counties Kerry and Cork – where such raising is widespread.

The phenomenon of nasal raising is not spectacular in itself and is found in many varieties of English, most notably in the Lower South of the United States. But a consideration of the history of Irish English shows that this raising was of a more general type previously. If one looks at the many literary satires which contain Irish English – for instance in the collection by Alan Bliss (1979) or in *A Corpus of Irish English* (Hickey 2003a) – then one sees that formerly the raising occurred in non-nasal environments as well, e.g. 'divil', 'togithir', (from Dion Boucicault's play *Arragh na Pogue*, 1864). What would appear to have happened in late 19th century, early 20th century Irish English is that the raising came to be restricted to environments in which it was phonetically natural, i.e. before nasals as these often trigger vowel raising due to their formant structure (Fry 1979: 118f.). This would mean that the situation in the south and south-west of Ireland is a remnant of a much wider occurrence of /ɛ/ → /ɪ/ raising.

A suprasegmental feature of the south, especially of the city of Cork is the large intonational range characterised by a noticeable drop in pitch on stressed syllables preceded by a rise on the preceding syllable. This intonational pattern is shared by Cork Irish, in the remnants which are still extant, so that this prosodic feature can be viewed as an areal feature of the south/south-west. The city of Cork also has a very open realisation of the vowels in the LOT and THOUGHT lexical sets which is seen in (often stereotypical) pronunciations of the city's name, [kaɹk].

A distinctive feature of the west is the use of dental stops in the THINK / BREATHE lexical sets. In vernacular varieties in the east and south, alveolar stops are employed here. In the history of Irish English one can assume that Irish speakers switching to English would have used the nearest equivalent to English /θ, ð/, i.e. the coronal stops of Irish. These stops were alveolar in the east and south, but dental in the west (de Bhaldraithe 1945) so that speakers used /t̪, d̪/ as equivalents to the English ambidental fricatives in their second language English. This dental pronunciation of the west has become that of the supraregional variety of Irish English, the latter deriving from usage in Dublin and spreading then throughout the country. But in colloquial Dublin English the realisation of ambidental fricatives has been as alveolar stops so it is not clear how vernacular speakers in Dublin came to use dental stops. One view is that they picked up this articulation from the many in-migrants into Dublin in the latter half of the 19th century, because it (i) allowed them to dissociate themselves phonetically from colloquial speakers in the city and (ii) permitted a reversal of homophony in word pairs such as *thinker* and *tinker*.

2.3. The Midlands

The centre of Ireland is a flat expanse bordered by the hills and mountains which occupy the coastal regions of the country (Mitchell 1976). In general the term 'Midlands' is used in Ireland to describe an area west of Co. Dublin as far as the Shannon and including its western shore linking up with east Clare, Galway and Mayo and on a north-south axis delimited by the border with Northern Ireland in the north and to the south by a line running roughly from Limerick across to Dublin. In this sense the Midlands actually refers to the north-central part of Ireland. Its extension to the south is limited and does not stretch far down into Co. Tipperary. The counties which are regarded as typically part of the Midlands are Westmeath, Longford, Offaly, Laois along with west Kildare and Meath, south Roscommon and north Tipperary. The main town in the Midlands is Athlone, situated on the Shannon about half way on its north-south course.

To the north, the Midlands show the transitional features of the north-south divide (Ó Baoill 1991) such as *u*-fronting, the use of dental fricatives for stops in the THINK / BREATHE lexical sets and a retroflex [ɻ] for the more traditional velarised [ɫ] of the south. The single most obvious feature of the Midlands is the shift of /tj/ to /k/ in intervocalic position as in *fortune* ['fɔrkuːn], already mentioned in the 19th century but by now highly recessive. Other features are shared by adjoining varieties.

Features of south and west from Cork through Limerick up to Galway and Mayo
/ɛ/ → /ɪ/ before nasals
Tense, raised articulation of /æ/ (also east)
Considerable intonational range (only south, south-west)
West
Dental stop realisation in THINK, BREATHE lexical sets
Low central onset for /ai/ and /au/, e.g. *quite* [kwaɪt], *town* [taʊn]
Midlands
Shift of /tj/ to /k/ in word-internal position, e.g. *fortune* ['fɔrkuːn]

3. Varieties of Northern Irish English

Any treatment of English in Ireland must take special account of the situation in Ulster. The reason for this lies in the settlement history of this province which led to the introduction of Scots and forms of northern English which were, and still are, distinct from all varieties of English in the south of the country. There has also been, as in the south, interaction between forms of English and Irish which has added a further dimension to the linguistic complexity in the north. A common means of alluding to the northern part of the island of Ireland is by the historical name 'Ulster' which covers the entire north of the country.

3.1. Terminology

Similarly to the south, any discussion of English in the north must begin with a consideration of terminology as there are many and frequently contradictory usages found in treatments of language in Ulster.

   Ulster English is both (i) a cover term for various forms of English used in Northern Ireland and (ii) a specific reference to English brought to Ulster from the north-west Midlands of England (Adams 1958: 61ff.) which is separate from the Scots element in the province. Because Ulster Scots (see next entry) is found in the peripheral counties of Ulster (Donegal, Derry, Antrim and Down – from west to east) the label 'Mid-Ulster English' (Harris 1984) is sometimes used to refer to general forms of English in Northern Ireland which are not derived from Scots.

   Ulster Scots A continuation of the Scots language brought to Ireland chiefly from the 17th century onwards (Adams (ed.) 1964, Montgomery 1997). Some tens of thousands of Scots arrived in the first half of this century and were mainly from the West-Mid and South-West Lowlands and show many of the features still typical of Scots.

   Northern Irish English subsumes all kinds of English in the north of the country, i.e. in all the nine countries of the province of Ulster and is used in the present chapter as a general term.

3.2. Ulster Scots

Of all the varieties stemming from English taken to Ireland since the 17th century, Ulster Scots is the only one which has retained a distinct profile and which can be unambiguously linked to the present-day varieties to which it is immediately related, Scots in western Scotland. Undoubtedly Ulster Scots – in its essentially rural forms – is quite separate from other varieties of English in the north of Ireland, let alone the south. Its divergent nature has meant that much debate has taken place concerning its status as a language or 'simply' a dialect, see the contributions in Kirk and Ó Baoill (eds) 2000.

The regions where Ulster Scots is spoken are nowadays no longer contiguous (the work reported on in Gregg 1972 was done over four decades ago). This would seem to imply a reduction of the previous geographical distribution. The areas where it is still found do, however, represent historical regions of settlement. There are three of these located on the northern periphery from north-west to north-east, hence the term 'Coastal Crescent' or 'Northern Crescent' (see map in section 1.1 *Dialect divisions* above).

3.3. Delimiting Ulster Scots

A treatment of Ulster Scots must start with differentiating between conservative Ulster Scots – 'braid', i.e. broad, Ulster Scots – which has its base in rural areas of Ulster and more standard forms which are spoken chiefly in urban centres, parallel to the established distinction in Scotland between, Lowland Scots and Scottish Standard English (Harris 1984: 119). An essential feature of non-local Ulster Scots (Gregg 1964) is that most words with non-standard Scots vowel values have re-allocated values which are nearer to those in general Ulster English. The following list illustrates vowel values and some consonantal features which are indicative of conservative Ulster Scots. The yardstick of reference is Older Scots (OS), up to 1700, i.e. before the emigration to Ulster began (Montgomery and Gregg 1997).

Features of conservative Ulster Scots
Retention of OS *ū* (not shifted to /au/) *cow* /kʉː/, *hoos* /hʉs/
A low, unrounded back vowel for OS *o*, *soft* /sɑːft/, *top* /tɑːp/
OS *ei* merges with /i/ and not /ai/ [əɪ, ɑe], *die* /diː/

OS *ō* has a fronted, unrounded reflex, *blood* /blɪd/
Fronting and raising of Old English *ā*, *home* /heːm/
Little raising of above vowel after labio-velars, *two* /tɔː/
Lowering of /ɪ/ to /ɛ/, *thick* /θɛk/
No raising of Middle English /ɛː/ to /iː/, *beat* /bet/, *meat* /met/
Raising of OS /a/ especially before /r/, *farm* /fɛːrm/
Distinct open and close mid back vowels, *horse* /hɔːrs/, *hoarse* /hoːrs/
Distinction between short vowels before /r/, *term* /tɛrm/, *burn* /bʌrn/
No rounding of /a/ after /w/, *swan* /swan/
Retention of distinction between /w/ and /ʍ/, *whale* /ʍeːl/, *wale* /weːl/
Retention of syllable-final /x/, *bought* /bɔːxt/, *enough* /ɪˈnʌx/
Vocalisation of word-final /l/ [ɫ], *full* /fʉː/, *wall* /wɔː/

The shifts of vowel values in Ulster Scots when compared to southern British English have led to a re-alignment of vowel space. This can best be indicated diagrammatically as follows. A major shift is that of Middle English /oː/ to a front vowel, with or without rounding, i.e. Older Scots /ɪ, ø/. In Ulster Scots this vowel appears as /ɪ/.

Ulster Scots vowel shifts			
/ɪ/	←	/oː/	*loom* /lɪm/
/æ/	←	/ɪ/	*limb* /læm/
/ɑː/	←	/æ/	*lamb* /lɑːm/

3.4. Contrasting northern and southern Irish English

In the following sections those features are discussed in which varieties in Ulster (both Ulster Scots and general Ulster English) differ from those south of the province. In a number of instances it is necessary to distinguish the two main groups within Ulster. The yardstick for the south is the supraregional standard which ultimately is derived from middle-class Dublin English of the mid 20th century.

Equivalents of ambidental fricatives In the entire area of Ulster the THINK and BREATHE lexical sets show fricatives. The only exception to this are areas of contact with Irish (in County Donegal) where one finds [t̪] and [d̪] because of the transfer from Irish of the realisations of /t/ and /d/ in the latter language.

	Ulster	*Supraregional Southern*
thick	[θɛk]	[t̪ɪk]
that	[ðat]	[d̪æt̪]
lather	[lɑː(ð)əɹ]	[laːd̪əɹ]
brother	[brʌ(ð)ər]	[brʌd̪əɹ]

Dentalisation of alveolar stops before /r/ This is a phonetic process whereby an alveolar stop – typically /t/ – is shifted forward to a dental point of articulation mostly when it is followed by an unstressed rhotic schwa. The /r/ is realised as a tap or slight trill due to the position of the tongue parallel to the escaping airstream (Bernoulli effect) and it frequently voiceless. The dentalisation can also be found before a stressed vowel, e.g. *trap* [t̪ræp], though here it appears to be less common.

	Ulster and Conservative Southern
water	[wɑːt̪ər]
better	[bɛt̪ər]

Allophones of alveolar plosives The fricativisation of /t/ and often /d/ intervocalically and word-finally before a pause is not generally to be found in the north – nor in other varieties of English, bar the Irish section of Newfoundland – and thus gains the status of a defining feature of southern Irish English. In Ulster, alveolar stops tend not to be released, above all when in final position.

	Ulster	Supraregional Southern
bat	[batˀ]	[bæt̯]
bead	[bidˀ]	[bid̯]

The palatalisation of velar plosives A conspicuous feature of northern Irish English is the palatalisation of /g/ and /k/ to /kj/ and /gj/ respectively. This palatalisation is only to be found before low vowels. It would appear to be an English and not a Scots feature and is attested in 18th century mainland English although it was later lost.

	Ulster	Supraregional Southern
cat	[kjat]	[kæt̯]
gap	[gjap]	[gæp]

Off-glides When mid front vowels occur in stressed position in northern Irish English then they tend to develop offglides. This is particularly clear before a following consonant.

	Ulster	Supraregional Southern
save	[seəv]	[seːv]
bait	[beət]	[beːt̯]

Unstressed vowels In unstressed positions southern Irish English frequently has the high vowel /i/ without the centralisation to [ɪ] which is found in RP, i.e. it shows so-called HAPPY-tensing. Northern Irish English tends to lower an unstressed /i/ to a value approaching /e/.

	Ulster	Supraregional Southern
tricky	[trĕke]	[trɪki]
happy	[hɑpe]	[hæpi]

Vowel quantity In Ulster, in strong contradistinction to the South, vowel quantity is often non-distinctive, particularly in areas with significant Ulster Scots concentrations. High and mid vowels, which are elsewhere either long or short, have half-long realisations.

	Ulster	*Supraregional Southern*
full	[fʉ·l]	[fʊl]
fool	[fʉ·l]	[fuːl]

3.5. Interpreting features of Irish English

In the history of Irish English studies the pendulum of opinion concerning the role of contact in the genesis of these forms of English has swung back and forth. Initially, writers like P. W. Joyce, P. L. Henry and, to a lesser extent, J. J. Hogan assumed that every feature which had a parallel in Irish was of Irish origin. This stance has been labelled the *substratist* position and came under heavy fire in the mid 1980s most noticeably in John Harris' influential article, Harris (1984). The *retentionist* standpoint, which saw the input varieties of English in early modern Ireland as the source of features hitherto accounted for by contact, came into vogue and was represented by various scholars, notably Roger Lass, e.g. Lass (1990). But in the 1990s the pendulum moved more to the centre with the gradual acceptance of contact as a source of specific features in Irish English (Hickey 1995). This resulted from a better understanding of the mechanisms of language transfer and language shift, not least due to authors on Irish English, such as Markku Filppula, taking on board the ideas of other linguists examining contact in general, expressed most clearly in the seminal monograph, Thomason and Kaufman (1988). Convergence became the new standard wisdom with contact and retention occupying places of equal standing in the history of Irish English. The following table offers suggestions for sources of key phonological features of Irish English.

Phonological feature	*Possible source*
Dental/alveolar stops for fricatives	Transfer of nearest Irish equivalent, i.e. coronal stops
Intervocalic and pre-pausal lenition of /t/	Lenition as a phonological directive from Irish

Alveolar /l/ in all positions	Use of non-velar, non-palatal [l] from Irish
Retention of [ʍ] for <*wh*>	Convergence of input with Irish /f/ [ɸ]
Retention of syllable-final /r/	Convergence of English input and Irish
Distinction of short vowels before /r/, e.g. *term* [tɛɹm] and *turn* [tʌɹn]	Convergence of English input and Irish
Epenthesis in heavy clusters in syllables codas, *film* [fɪləm]	Areal feature of both Irish and English in Ireland
U-fronting in the north, e.g. *boot* [bʉt]	Areal feature of both Irish and English in Ulster
Lowering of short front vowels, e.g. *bit* [bet]	Input to Ulster from Scotland
Use of retroflex *r* in Ulster	Input to Ulster from Scotland

3.6. Ireland as a linguistic area

The above table contains features which are traits of different vernacular varieties found throughout the entire island. However, when treating features of Irish English a holistic view can be useful, that is, rather than stress differences, one could examine the features common to most or all varieties and indeed go a step further and compare these to parallel structures in Irish. This approach is largely typological and sees Ireland (north and south) as a linguistic area (Hickey 1999a). Not all of these are strongly diagnostic of Ireland as a linguistic area as they are also found in forms English in England, quite apart from anglophone varieties overseas. One should also mention that the non-existence of features across the entire country has led to negative definers for Irish English arising. For instance *r*-lessness and/or *h*-dropping are definite signs that a speaker is not Irish. In order to underline the significance of areal features of English in Ireland, morphological and syntactic features are included below.

Table 1. Shared features in vernacular varieties of Irish English

---

Phonology

1) Lenition or tap realisation of alveolar stops in positions of high sonority, e.g. *city* ['sɪt̬i] / ['sɪɾi]
2) Use of clear [l] in all positions in a word (only in conservative varieties)
3) Retention of syllable-final /r/
4) Distinction of short vowels before /r/ (only in conservative varieties)
5) Retention of the distinction between /ʍ/ and /w/
6) Frequent merger or allophonic conditioning of vowels in TRAP and BATH lexical sets.

Morphology

1) Distinction between second singular and plural personal pronouns
2) Epistemic negative *must*, e.g. *He mustn't be Scottish.*
3) *Them* as demonstrative, e.g. *Them shoes in the hall.*

Syntax

1) Perfective aspect with two sub-types:
    a) Immediate perfective, e.g. *She is after spilling the milk.*
    b) Resultative perfective, e.g. *She has the housework done.* (OV word order)
2) Habitual aspect, expressed by *do + be* or *bees* or inflectional *-s* in the first person singular:
    a) *She does be reading books.*
    b) *They bees up late at night.*
    c) *I gets awful anxious about the kids when they're away.*
3) Reduced number of verb forms, e.g. *seen* and *done* as preterite, *went* as past participle
4) Negative concord, e.g. *He's not interested in no cars.*
5) Clefting for topicalisation purposes, e.g. *It's to Glasgow he's going.*
6) Greater range of the present tense, e.g. *I know him for more than six years now.*

7) *Be* as auxiliary, e.g. *They're finished the work now.*
8) *Till* in the sense of 'in order that', e.g. *Come here till I tell you.*
9) Singular time reference for *never*, e.g. *She never rang yesterday evening.*
10) *For to* infinitives of purpose, e.g. *He went to Dublin for to buy a car.* (only in conservative varieties)
11) Subordinating *and* (frequently concessive), e.g. *We went for a walk and it raining.* (only in conservative varieties)
12) Preference for *that* as relative pronoun, e.g. *This is the book that I read.*
13) Retention of interrogative word order in indirect questions, e.g. *I don't know will she come* 'I don't know if she will come'.

---

4.   Urban English in Ireland

4.1. English in Dublin

The English language has been spoken in Dublin since the late 12th century. English never died out in the capital and there are some features of colloquial Dublin English which can be traced to the first period (Hickey 2002). The records of Dublin English are slight and consist before 1600 mainly of municipal records which here and there betray the kind of English which must have been spoken in the city (Henry 1958). For an historical background to present-day speech one must look to the elocutionist Thomas Sheridan (the father of the playwright Richard Brinsley Sheridan) who in 1781 published *A Rhetorical Grammar of the English Language* with an appendix in which he commented on the English used by middle class Dubliners, the 'gentlemen of Ireland' in his words, which he regarded as worthy of censure on his part. When discussing consonants Sheridan remarks on 'the thickening (of) the sounds of *d* and *t* in certain situations'. Here he is probably referring to the realisation of ambidental fricatives as alveolar plosives as found in colloquial forms of Dublin English today. There is no hint in Sheridan of anything like a distinction between dental and alveolar plosive realisations, which is a marker of local versus non-local speech in Dublin today.

Local Dublin	Non-local Dublin
thank, tank [tæŋk]	*thank* [t̪æŋk], *tank* [tæŋk]

Any discussion of English in Dublin necessitates a few basic divisions into types. For the present contribution a twofold division, with a further subdivision, is employed. The first group consists of those who use the inherited popular form of English in the capital. The term 'local' is intended to capture this and to emphasise that these speakers are those who show strongest identification with traditional conservative Dublin life of which the popular accent is very much a part. The reverse of this is 'non-local' which refers to sections of the metropolitan population who do not wish a narrow, restrictive identification with popular Dublin culture. This group then subdivides into a larger, more general section, 'mainstream', and a currently smaller group which vigorously rejects a confining association with low-prestige Dublin. For want of a better term, this group is labelled 'fashionable'. It should be stressed that the pronunciations which are typical of this variety are shifting into the mainstream as more and more speakers adopt the new pronunciation. Indeed many of the features which were typical of new, fashionable Dublin English 15 years ago are characteristic of the mainstream variety today, at least for the younger generation.

Forms of English in present-day Dublin		
1) *local Dublin English*		
2) *non-local Dublin English*	– a)	*mainstream Dublin English*
	b)	*new Dublin English*

A central issue in contemporary Dublin English is the set of vowel shifts which represent the most recent phonological innovation in Irish English (see section 4.1.2. *Recent developments* below). This is not surprising as Dublin is a typical location for language change given the following features. 1) The city has expanded greatly in population in the last three or four decades. The increase in population has been due both to internal growth and migration into the city from the rest of the country. 2) It has undergone an economic boom in the last 15 years or so, reflected in its position as an important financial centre and as a location for many computer firms which run their European operations from Dublin. The increase in wealth and international position has meant that many young people aspire to an urban sophistication which is divorced from strongly local Dublin life. For this reason the developments in fashionable Dublin English diverge from those in local Dublin English, indeed can be interpreted as a reaction to it. This type of linguistic behaviour can be termed *local dissociation* as it is motivated by the desire of speakers to hive themselves off from vernacular forms of a variety spoken in their immediate surroundings (Hickey 1999b).

4.1.1. Features of local Dublin English

Vowel breaking Long high vowels are sometimes realised as two syllables with a hiatus between the two when they occur in closed syllables. The hiatus element is [j] with front vowels and [w] with back vowels, *clean* [kliʲən], *fool* [fuʷəl]. The disyllabification of long high vowels extends to diphthongs with a high end point as can be seen in the following realisations: *time* [təʲəm], *pound* [pɛʷən]. Among the further prominent vocalic characteristics of Dublin English are the following: (1) Fronting of /au/, e.g. *down* [dæun] – [dɛun], (2) Lengthening of historically short vowels before /r/, e.g. *circle* [seːkl̩], *first* [fuːs(t)], (3) Retention of early modern English short /u/, e.g. *Dublin* [dublən].

    Cluster simplification Stops after fricatives or sonorants are liable to deletion. Intermediate registers may have a glottal stop as a trace of the stop in question: *pound* [pɛun(ʔ)], *last* [læːs(ʔ)].

    Fortition of dental fricatives It is safe to assume that the realisation in popular Dublin English of the THINK and BREATHE lexical sets with the alveolar plosives – [t] and [d] respectively – is not a recent phenomenon. Hogan (1927: 71f.) notes that it is found in the seventeenth century plays (assuming that *t, d* represent [t, d]) and furthermore in the Dublin City Records (from the first period, i.e. before the 17th century, see above) where the third person singular ending *-th* appears as *-t*.

    T-*lenition* A significant phonetic feature of southern Irish English is the realisation in weak positions of /t/ as a fricative with identical characteristics of the stop, i.e. as an apico-alveolar fricative. Extensions include the lenition beyond the initial stage of apico-alveolar fricative to /r/ then to /h/ with final deletion as in the following instance.

Cline of t-lenition in Dublin English			
/t/	[t̪] →	[ɹ] →	[h] → ø
water	[wɑːt̪ər]	[wɑːɹər]	[wɑːhər] [wɑːər]

4.1.2. Recent developments

In present-day Ireland the major instance of language change is undoubtedly the shift in pronunciation of Dublin English. To understand the workings of this shift one must realise that in the course of the 1980s and 1990s the city of Dublin, as the capital of the Republic of Ireland, underwent a considerable expansion in population size and in relative prosperity with a great increase in international connections to and from the metropolis. The in-migrants to the city, who arrived there chiefly to avail of the job opportunities resulting from the economic boom formed a group of socially mobile, weak-tie speakers and their section of the city's population has been a key locus for language change. The change which arose in the last two decades of the 20th century was reactive in nature: fashionable speakers began to move away in their speech from their perception of popular Dublin English, a classic case of dissociation in an urban setting (Hickey 2000a).

The variable (ai) in Irish English A conservative pronunciation in Dublin of (ai) as [əɪ] is maintained in lower-class speech whereas the supraregional variety of the south has for (ai) a diphthong which has a low mid or low front starting point, i.e., either [aɪ] or [æɪ]. For non-local Dubliners the [aɪ, æɪ] pronunciations sufficiently delimit them from local Dublin English. But increasingly a back starting-point came to be used with this diphthong. This retracted starting-point is particularly noticeable before /r/ so that the name of the country can be realised as [ɑɹlənd] rather than [aɹlənd]. The status of this retraction is uncertain among younger non-regional speakers in Ireland. It is not favoured by all and the retraction may now (2004) be associated either with a rather English pronunciation – reminiscent of Received Pronunciation (henceforth: RP) and thus to be avoided – or with the now dated 'Dublin 4' accent of the 1980s (the name derives from the postal number of a upmarket district in the immediate south of Dublin). In the many recordings of younger female speakers from Dublin in the sound atlas one can note that /ai/-retraction is by no means universal whereas the raising of the low back vowels (see next paragraph) is very widespread.

Summary of the present-day vowel shift

Retraction of diphthongs with a low or back starting point

time	[taɪm]	→	[tɑɪm]
toy	[tɒɪ]	→	[tɔ˞ɪ], [toɪ]

Raising of low back vowels

cot	[kɒt̪]	→	[kɔt̪]
caught	[kɒːt̪]	→	[kɔ˞ːt̪], [koːt̪]
Cork	[kɒːɹk]	→	[kɔ˞ːɹk], [koːɹk]

(ai) *retraction*   aɪ   →   ɑɪ

Low back vowel	oɪ		oː
raising	↑		↑
	ɔɪ	ɔ	ɔː
	↑	↑	↑
	ɒɪ	ɒ	ɒː

General shift of low vowels The vowel shift in Dublin English is not just confined to the realisation of (ai). Other vowels are affected, particularly the diphthong in the CHOICE lexical set and the low and mid vowels in the LOT and THOUGHT sets. In traditional mainstream Irish English these vowels have a lower realisation than in Britain (or unrounded in the case of the LOT vowel), *choice* /tʃɔɪs/ → [tʃɒɪs], *lot* /lɒt/ → [lɒt̪] - [lat̪], *thought* /ɔː/ → [t̪ɒːt̪]. Raised realisations of these vowels, stemming from the vowel shift which originated in Dublin, are now common among all young people, e.g. *choice* /tʃɔɪs/ → [tʃɔ˞ɪs], [tʃoɪs]. Such realisations are especially prominent before /r/ where the high vowel is combined with a retroflex [ɹ], yielding a pronunciation far removed from more traditional realisations, e.g. *fork*, traditional: [fɒːɹk], new: [foːɻk]. The new pronunciation in southern Irish English is a change has the characteristics of a chain shift, that is, it affects several segments by a process of retraction and raising in phonological vowel space. This can be seen from the following table below which summarise the main vowel developments.

4.1.3. The spread of the new Dublin accent

Because of the status of Dublin in the Republic of Ireland, non-vernacular speech of the capital acts as a *de facto* standard for the rest of the south when speakers, outside of Dublin, are seeking a non-local, generally acceptable form of Irish English. This has also meant, for instance, that the retroflex [ɻ], which has become common in Dublin, is spreading out of the capital with the younger generation from different parts of the country. This dissemination of new Dublin English has particularly affected young females throughout the south of Ireland. For the following discussion, this speech is labelled the New Pronunciation, the capital letters deliberately suggesting a bundle of features which are adopted as a group by young speakers.

Apart from vowels, the New Pronunciation of southern Irish English involves above all the realisation of the liquids /l/ and /r/. Other segments do not seem to be affected by the shift in pronunciation. Specifically, the complex area of coronal segments (Hickey 1984) has not been altered to any significant extent. In addition to (*ai) retraction* and *low back vowel raising* (see table above), one can note the following features.

1) */au/-fronting* In Dublin English, and indeed in traditional east-coast varieties of Irish English in general (Hickey 2001), the vowel in the MOUTH lexical set has a front starting point, either [æ] or [ɛ]. A realisation as [au] is more conservative in Dublin and in rural areas it is traditionally typical of the south-west and west of Ireland, but is being replaced by the fronted realisation in the speech of the younger generation.

2) *SOFT-lengthening* Here one is again dealing with a traditional feature of Dublin English. The vowel of the LOT lexical set, when it occurs before a voiceless fricative, is lengthened. This long vowel used to be

characteristic of southern British English but was replaced by a short vowel. Dublin English kept the earlier long vowel which is in keeping with the general Early Modern English lengthening of Middle English /a/ before such fricatives which can be still seen in words like *staff, pass, path* in southern British English (Wells 1982: 203-6). In conservative mainstream Irish English, SOFT-lengthening (to use a cover term with a typical word involving this lengthening) is not found, but again because it is present in Dublin English, it is spreading to the rest of the country.

3) */r/-retroflexion* Traditionally, the realisation of /r/ in southern Irish English is a velarised alveolar continuant. As this pronunciation is found in western and south-western varieties of Irish to this day it can be assumed that this type of /r/ resulted in Irish English from transfer of the Irish realisation of the same phoneme (Hickey 1986a). In Northern Ireland, a retroflex /r/ is to be found, a parallel with Scotland, which may well have been the source for this realisation. In new Dublin English a retroflex /r/ is also to be found, though independently of its occurrence in Northern Ireland as varieties of English there have played no role in the shaping of Dublin English. Dissociation from the traditional velarised realisation of /r/ in southern Irish English and/or from the low rhoticity of popular Dublin English are likely reasons for the rise of the retroflex [ɻ] which has become widespread throughout Ireland among younger speakers, above all females. The combination of retroflex [ɻ] and vowel raising is something which many people have become conscious of (though not as an awareness of a general vowel shift). At the present (2004) one can hear comments on such prominent pronunciations as [koːɻk] for *Cork* which in conservative mainstream Irish English would still be pronounced [kɒːɹk].

Non-regional speakers – both in Dublin and outside the capital – may also show a slightly raised /aː/ – [æ(ː)], [æ˕(ː)] (the realisations need not be phonetically long) – in the START lexical set which co-occurs with the retroflexion of /r/ so that one has pronunciations like [stæ˕(ː)ɻt] for *start*.

4) */l/-velarisation* Traditionally, Irish English has an alveolar [l] in all syllable positions (Hickey 1986a). However, the recordings for young female speakers in the sound atlas overwhelmingly show a clear velarisation of /l/ in this position, e.g. *field* [fiːᵊɫd]. The development of [ɫ] could be seen as a reaction to the traditional alveolar [l] so long a prominent feature of Irish accents.

Apart from the above six features there are others which play a minor role in the sound profile of the New Pronunciation. One obvious feature of local Dublin English which has avoided stigma and hence is found in fashionable speech in the city is the loss of /hw/ [ʍ] in words like *whale, while* and which leads to mergers of pairs like *which* and *witch.* Traditionally, the occurrence of [ʍ] in all words beginning with *wh* is a prominent feature of Irish English (Hickey 1984), but if the New Pronunciation establishes itself in the next generation as the new supra-regional form of Irish English then this will no longer be the case.

4.2. English in Belfast

The area of contemporary Belfast is characterised by a conurbation which stretches along the north shore of Belfast Lough at least to Newtownabbey in County Antrim and on the south shore at least to Holywood in County Down. Along the Lagan Valley the city stretches to the south-west at least to Lisburn with a motorway to the triad of towns Lurgan, Craigavon, Portadown to the south of Lough Neagh. The Lagan Valley is the hinterland of Belfast and there is a similarity between accents in the city and those in its hinterland to the south-west. In general one can say that Lagan Valley speech is similar to the accents in West Belfast. The east of the city shows greater similarity with accents from rural North Down, an originally Scots area of settlement as opposed to Lagan Valley which was largely settled from northern England.

4.2.1. Sources of Belfast English

The English spoken in Belfast is an amalgam of features which come from the two main English communities in Ulster with independent traits only found in the capital city. The following is a list of features which can be clearly attributed to one of the two main English-language sources in Ulster (J. Milroy 1981: 25f.).

Ulster Anglo-Irish features in Belfast English (after Milroy 1981)
Palatalisation of /k, g/ before /a/, /kjat/ for *cat*
Dentalisation of /t, d/ before /r/, /bɛt̪ə/ for *better*
Unrounding of /ɒ/, /pɑt/ for *pot*
ME /ɛː/ realised as a mid-vowel, /bɛːt/ for *beat*
Lowering of /ɛ/ to /æ/, *set* /sæt/
The use of /au/ before /l/ in monosyllables, /aul/ for *old* also a feature of Lowland Scots.

Ulster Scots features in Belfast English (after Milroy 1981)
Raising of /æ/ to /ɛ/ before velars, /bɛk, bɛg/ for *back, bag*
Raising of /æ/ to /ɛ/ after /k/ and (residually) /g/ /kɛp, kɛsl̩/ for *cap, castle*
Short realisations of high vowels, /bit, bʉt/ for *beet, boot*
Lowering and sometimes centralisation of /ɪ/, /bɛt, sɛns/ or /bʌt, sʌns/ for *bit, since*

The sociolinguistic developments in Belfast English, which were described in ground-breaking studies by James and Lesley Milroy in terms of social networks in the 1970s and early 1980s, are outside the scope of the present study, for appropriate references, consult the relevant sections of Hickey (2002).

Mention should also be made of the distinct intonational patterns in northern Irish English. In her study Rahilly (1997) notes a general predominance of rises in intonation in Belfast which contrast explicitly with falls in the south of Britain. Indeed the high numbers of rising nuclei and level tails in tone sequences are regarded as typical of 'the Anglo-Irish group of dialects' rather than the 'British group'. Rahilly concludes that the primary cue to prominence in Belfast is a high pitch, but with much less movement than with nuclei in RP.

4.3. English in Derry

The city of Derry has a population of over 95,000 (1991 census) and is ethnically over 70% Catholic as opposed to Belfast which has a majority Protestant population. There is a large degree of segregation in terms of residence for the two communities: east of the River Foyle, which divides the city, Protestants are found while the area west of the river is almost exclusively Catholic. The segregation has increased greatly in the last 30 years or so because of the sectarian violence which lasted into the mid 1990s.

The only research on the English of Derry city is that of McCafferty (see various references), apart from one study of intonation in Derry (McElholm 1986). The city has a special status within Northern Ireland as it is on the one hand the second largest and on the other the only major city with a Catholic majority. It is understandable that it would receive innovations which stem from Belfast but also that the Catholic majority in the city might well show an inherent resistance to these. A number of changes are recorded for Derry which are listed in the following.

Four major linguistic changes in Derry English
1) A gradual replacement of [ʌ] by the [ʉ] of general Northern Irish English (NIE) which has been ongoing in Ulster for some time.
2) A widespread vernacular innovation, originating in the east of Northern Ireland, which replaces older [ɪ] by [iə] in the FACE class (both of these alternate with the [e] of general Northern Irish English).
3) A vernacular innovation that appears to have originated in the east in the last hundred years by which intervocalic [ð] is deleted.
4) A local Derry English innovation which realises the same intervocalic [ð] as a lateral [l].

Variable	General NIE	Older General Derry	Recent Local Derry	Lexical set
(ʌ)	[ʉ]	[ʌ]	[ʉ]	PULL
(e)	[e]	[ɪ]	[iə]	FACE
(ð)	[ð]	0	[l]	OTHER

Changes according to ethnicity McCafferty (1999, 2001) maintains that there is a tendency for the SQUARE and NURSE lexical sets to merge, a feature spreading from the east of Northern Ireland and typical of the Protestant middle class. For this group a lack of quantity distinctions with the NORTH and FORCE lexical sets is also found. The shift of older [ɪ] to [iə] in the FACE class is taken to be characteristic of younger Protestants. Protestant changes are in general incoming innovations which are spreading from eastern Northern Ireland, i.e. from the Belfast conurbation. In this case the changes for the Protestants in Derry have arisen through a process of supraregionalisation of Belfast innovations. The only *leading* change among the Catholics in Derry is the shift of intervocalic [ð] to a lateral [l]. Protestants in Derry would not appear to have vernacular innovations of their own.

Changes in Derry English according to ethnicity		
Ethnic group		*Source*
Protestants [oːr] → [ɔːr]		Eastern Northern Ireland
[ɛr] → [əːr]		–
[eɪ] → [ɪə]		–
Catholics [- ð -] → [- l -]		Local to Derry city

5.   Data categories for Irish English

5.1. Lexical sets for Irish English

To facilitate orientation and to make the data easily comparable to that for other varieties of English, the established practice of using lexical sets was chosen for the sound atlas project. A lexical set consists of a group of words all of which have the same pronunciation for a certain sound in a given variety. For instance, the lexical set TRAP is used to refer to the pronunciation which speakers of a variety have for the sound which is /æ/ in RP. So if speakers use [a] or [ɛ] in TRAP it is taken that they will use [a] or [ɛ] in all other words which contain this vowel, e.g. *bad, latter, shall*, i.e. in the words which comprise the lexical set. The advantage of this is that instead of saying the realisation of the /æ/ vowel in variety X, which phonetically can be quite far removed from [æ], one can refer to the vowel in the lexical set TRAP. The keyword of a lexical set is written in SMALL CAPITALS.

   The original group of lexical sets was presented in John C. Wells' three volume work *Accents of English* (Cambridge University Press, 1982). These were intended to cover the vowels of RP and their realisations in accents of English throughout the world. However, it became increasingly apparent that the group was not sufficient to deal with the phonetic distinctions present in many forms of English outside England. For instance, in many varieties of present-day Irish English it is necessary to have a lexical set PRICE and PRIDE as the realisations of the /ai/ diphthong varies according to the value for [voice] of the segment which follows it. There may also be historical distinctions present in varieties of English which have been lost in more mainstream varieties of English. These then require additional lexical sets, for instance, in local Dublin English originally short high vowels before tautosyllabic /r/, and back vowels after /w/ in the same position, have developed into a vowel which is phonetically something like [uː], e.g. *first* [fuː(ɹ)st], *turn* [tuː(ɹ)n], *work* [wuː(ɹ)k]. However, originally mid front vowels in this position are realised by [ɛː], e.g. *germ* [gɛː(ɹ)m], thus merging with the vowel realisation in the SQUARE lexical set. Because of this, Wells NURSE lexical set is represented by two such sets in the present study, NURSE illustrating the [ʊ:] pronunciation and TERM showing the [ɛ:] realisation.

Wells' group of lexical sets only refer to vowel values. But of course the variation among consonants across forms of English is considerable so for the sound atlas various consonantal lexical sets were devised and included. The relevant consonant in such lexical sets is indicated by underlining, e.g. WHICH which refers to the use of [ʍ] or [w] at the beginning of this word and all others like it. Again the usefulness of lexical sets is immediately obvious here: for varieties of English in the Republic of Ireland (as opposed to those in Northern Ireland) it makes little sense to talk of the realisation of /θ/ or /ð/ because so many speakers never have either [θ] or [ð], rather the possibilities range between a dental and alveolar stop, i.e. [t̪, d̪] or [t, d]. For this reason, the lexical sets THINK and BREATHE have been introduced to refers to sounds which in more mainstream varieties of English are [θ] and [ð] respectively.

Vocalic lexical sets based on Wells 1982, adapted to Irish English
  (phonetic values given are those of traditional mainstream varieties)

Short vowels		Long vowels		Rising diphthongs	
KIT	/ɪ/	FLEECE	/i:/	PRICE/PRIDE	/ai/
DRESS	/e/	FACE	/e:/	MOUTH	/au/
TRAP	/æ/	BATH	/a:/	CHOICE	/ɒi/
LOT	/ɒ/	DANCE	/a:/	GOAT	/ou/
STRUT	/ʌ/	THOUGHT	/ɒ:/		
FOOT	/ʊ/	GOOSE	/u:/		
SOFT	/ɒ/				

Rhotacised and unstressed vowels

Centring vowels		Low + back vowels		Unstressed vowels	
NEAR	/iɚ/	START	/ɑ:r/	LETTER	/-ɚ/
SQUARE	/eɚ/	NORTH	/ɒ:r/	COMMA	/-ə/
CURE	/uɚ/	FORCE	/o:r/	HAPPY	/-i/

NURSE	/ɚː/		
TERM	/ɚː/		

Consonantal lexical sets (for southern and northern Irish English)

Dental stops/ fricatives	Alveolar stops (initial)	Alveolar stops (medial)	Alveolar stops (final)
THINK /t̪ θ/	TWO /t-/	WATER /-t-/	GET /-t/
BREATHE /d̪ ð/	DIP /d-/	READY /-d-/	SAID /-d/

L-sounds	R-sounds
RAIL /-l/	RUN /r-/
LOOK /l-/	SORE /-r/

Velar stops	Velar nasal
GAP /g-/	TALKING /-ŋ/
CAP /k-/	

Alveolar and alveolo-palatal sibilants
SHOES   /ʃ-z/

Voiced labio-velar approximant	Voiceless labio-velar approx.
WET /w-/	WHICH /hw-/ [ʍ]

The words with which Wells chose to illustrate his lexical sets are sometimes not very common. For instance, the lexical set which contains the /ʌ/ vowel of RP is STRUT. However, the word *strut* does not occur anywhere in the recordings of Irish English which the present author has collected over the past decade or so, let alone occur in a form suitable for a digital recording. This means that the sound files on the DVD which illustrate various lexical sets may contain pronunciations of some other word, e.g. *cut* for the STRUT lexical set (in the sample sentence *He cut the piece of twine*). The same is true of the FLEECE lexical set. This was tested by using the word *meet* in the sample sentence *They didn't bother to meet him.*

The following tables use the lexical sets as originally introduced by John Wells in the early 1980s and adapted as outlined above. The five columns in each table correspond to a small selection of varieties which represent some main types of Irish English. The phonetic realisations, indicated by the transcriptions below, can be heard on the DVD by selecting the option *Maps with transcriptions* in the branch *Sound Atlas – first approach* to be seen in the tree of the Java version of the sound atlas processing software (for details see section III *Processing software for atlas data*, 1.1. *Java version* below).

Vocalic sets

Lexical set	Rural North	Popular Dublin	Fashion. Dublin	Rural SW-West	Supr. Southern
KIT	e	ɪ	ɪ	ɪ	ɪ
DRESS	ɛ˕	ɛ	ɛ	ɛ	ɛ
TRAP	a	æ	æ	æ	æ
LOT	ɒ	ɑ	ɒ	ɑ	ɑ
STRUT	ʌ	ʊ	ʌ̈	ʌ̈	ʌ̈
FOOT	ʉ	ʊ	ʊ	ʊ	ʊ
FLEECE	i	iː(ə)	iː	iː	iː
FACE	eə	eː	eː	eː	eː
BATH	ɑ(ː)	æː	aː	æ(ː)	aː
THOUGHT	ɔ(ː)	ɒː	ɔːˑ, oː	ɑː	ɒː
SOFT	ɔ(ː)	ɒː	ɔːˑ	ɒ	ɒ
GOOSE	ʉ(ː)	uːˑ	uːˑ	uː	uː
PRICE	ɛɪ	əɪ	a/ɑɪ	æɪ	aɪ
PRIDE	ɛɪ	əɪ	ɑɪ	aɪ	aɪ
MOUTH	ɛʉ	ɛʊ	ɛʊ	aʊ	æʊ
CHOICE	ɔɪ	ɑɪ	ɔɪ, oɪ	ɑɪ	ɒɪ
GOAT	oʊ, oː	ʌɔ	əʊ	oː	oʊ, oː
NEAR	i(ː)ɻ	iː(ɹ)	iːɻ	iːɹ	iːɹ

SQUARE	ɛ-(ː)ɻ	ɛː(ɨ)	eˑɻ (øˑɻ)	eːɨ	eːɨ
START	ɑ(ː)ɻ	aː(ɨ)	aˑɻ/ɑˑɻ	a(ː)ɨ	ɑːɨ
NORTH	ɔ(ː)ɻ	ɑː(ɨ)	oˑɻ	ɑːɨ	ɒːɨ
FORCE	o(ː)ɻ	oː(ɨ)	oˑɻ	oːɨ	oːɹ
CURE	u(ː)ɻ	uːə(ɨ)	uˑɻ	uːɨ	uːɨ
NURSE	ə(ː)ɻ	əː-(ɨ)	ɚˑ+	ɚː	ɚː
COMMA	ə	ə, ɐ	ə	ə	ə
LETTER	əɻ	ə(ɨ)	əɻ	ɚ	ɚ
HAPPY	ɪ, e	i	i	i	i
DANCE	a	æ(ː)	a(ː)	æ(ː)	a(ː)
PATH	ɑ(ː)	æː	aː	æ(ː)	aː

Remarks

1)   The vowel values which are associated with the now unfashionable 'Dublin 4' accent are not shared entirely by younger non-local Dublin English speakers. In particular the retraction of /aː/, and the raising of the rhotacised version /ɑːɹ/, is avoided so that the earlier pronunciation of *Dart* as [dɔːɹt / doːɹt] is regarded as 'uncool'.

2)   The vowel transcribed as [ʌ] is a slightly centralised version of the corresponding cardinal vowel.

3)   The realisation [øːɹ] in the SQUARE lexical set can be interpreted as a reaction to the very open, unrounded realisation of popular Dublin English as in *term* [tɛː(ɨ)m].

4)   Popular Dublin English is weakly rhotic and early conservative forms of this form are often entirely non-rhotic.

5)   There is a complex distribution of low vowels in northern Irish English. Basically one can say that a front and raised vowel is found before velars and a retracted variant before labials and nasals, giving typical pronunciations like *bag* [bɛ₊g] and *family* ['famlɪ].

Consonantal sets

Lexical set	Rural Northern	Popular Dublin	Fashion. Dublin	Rural SW-West	Supr. Southern
TH<u>I</u>NK	θ	t	t̪	t	t̪
BREA<u>THE</u>	ð	d	d̪	d	d̪
<u>T</u>WO	t	t	t, tˢ	t	t
WA<u>T</u>ER	ɾ, ʔ, Ø	ʔ, h, Ø	ɾ, t̪	t̞	t̪ (ɾ)
GE<u>T</u>	t˺, ʔ	h, Ø	t̞	t̞	t̞
FEE<u>L</u>	ɫ, Ø	l, ɬ	ɬ	l	l (ɬ)
SO<u>R</u>E	ɻ	ɹ, Ø	ɻ	ɹ	ɹ (ɻ)
<u>W</u>ET	w	w	w	w	w
<u>WH</u>ICH	w, ʍ	w, ʍ	w (ʍ)	ʍ	ʍ (w)

Remarks

1) The distinction between dental and alveolar stops is sociolinguistically significant in Ireland. All speakers can hear this difference clearly and the use of alveolar for dental stops in the THINK and BREATHE lexical sets is stigmatised.

2) Fashionable Dublin English speakers may have a slight affrication of syllable-initial /t-/ as in *two* [tˢuː].

3) The allophony of syllable-coda and intersyllabic /t/ is quite complicated. With conservative supraregional speakers the apico-alveolar fricative [t̞] is found. With younger supraregional speakers a flap can be found. In popular Dublin English the lenition of /t/ continues through a glottal stop to /h/ and frequently to zero, especially in word-final position. In many forms of northern Irish English, final alveolar stops may be unreleased.

4) The merger of [w] and [ʍ] is increasingly frequent with supraregional speakers so that for many word pairs like *which* and *witch* may now consists of homophones.

5)   It is merely a coincidence that fashionable Dublin English shares a flap (ɾ) and a retroflex *r* (ɻ) with northern Irish English.

5.2. Sample sentences used for *A Sound Atlas of Irish English*

The following sentences were read by all the informants and forms the basis for the sound atlas. Speakers were asked to read the sentences 'in their normal voice'. The sentences contain all the lexical sets for the vowels and consonants of Irish English (see charts of lexical sets above), along with some which are intended to provide information about special aspects of speakers' pronunciation, e.g. whether they used a velarised *l* or where they placed stress in certain polysyllabic words (verbs with heavy final syllables). The sentences they were shown did not have the keywords in uppercase (as in the list here) so that speakers had no idea what type of pronunciation was being checked.

They bought a KIT to make beer.	I suppose they're HAPPY now.
She bought herself a new DRESS.	She's learning how to DANCE.
They walked into the TRAP.	We took a different PATH.
There're a LOT of people outside.	I THINK it's time to go.
He CUT the piece of twine.	Now BREATHE in slowly, please.
He put his FOOT in it.	There're TWO of them here.
They didn't bother to MEET him.	She'd like to go for a DIP.
You have to put a brave FACE on it.	They've a new WATER supply.
They bought a new BATH last week.	Are they READY now?
Spare a THOUGHT for your parents.	Will you GET another chance?
You should go SOFT on him.	She SAID she was coming.

They kept a G<u>OO</u>SE in the back yard.	Take a <u>L</u>OOK at the car.
The PR<u>ICE</u> has gone up again.	The RAI<u>L</u> track is overgrown.
They're the PR<u>IDE</u> of the nation.	You'll have to <u>R</u>UN for the bus.
The city is at the M<u>OU</u>TH of the river.	My back is very SO<u>RE</u> lately.
The CH<u>OI</u>CE was the right one.	There's a <u>G</u>AP in the field.
They had a G<u>OA</u>T on their farm.	He put his <u>C</u>AP on.
It's near the M<u>O</u>DERN station.	He was TALK<u>ING</u> about his wife.
Down by the town SQ<u>UARE</u>.	She took her <u>SH</u>OES off.
There's a C<u>URE</u> for that now.	The whole floor is <u>W</u>ET.
The film should ST<u>AR</u>T soon.	<u>WH</u>ICH one do you mean?
He's travelling up NO<u>R</u>TH.	That wasn't V<u>E</u>RY F<u>AIR</u>. /-eri, -e:r/
The F<u>O</u>RCE of the wind increased.	It's just his ST<u>YLE</u>. /-ail/
Ask the other NU<u>R</u>SE for water.	We haven't any T<u>IME</u>. /-aim/
The prison T<u>ER</u>M was quite long.	They REAL<u>ISE</u>D the problem.
There's a LETT<u>ER</u> for you today.	We live in <u>IRE</u>LAND. /air-/
Put a COMM<u>A</u> after that word.	All of us are <u>IR</u>ISH. /air-/

5.3. Free text used for recordings

The following short text was read by about one quarter of the informants (depending on their readiness to do this and the inherent interest of the author in their pronunciation). Speakers were asked to read it casually at their normal rate of speech. The text contains nearly all the sounds which are in the sample sentences as well, but as these are embedded in this piece of free text, the pronunciation was slightly less formal for many speakers.

Getting ready for their holidays

Michael and Maura had been planning to go to Italy for a long time now. First they were thinking of going in July but decided that it would be too hot. They also realised that there're too many tourists around then. Instead they thought they'd travel at a quieter time, like early spring, so they booked their flight for March. The travel agency was able to fix up a nice apartment for them to stay in. This meant they could drive around during the day and not be tied to mealtimes in a hotel. The plane was to fly from Dublin to Rome and the idea was that someone on the other side was to pick them up and take them to the apartment. Maura wanted to go for a whole month, but Michael thought a fortnight was enough. After all, he said, they could always come again if they liked it. Maura was thinking she might learn some Italian. It was a soft language she said, it sounded like music, and she worked out that she could do an hour every morning, listening to tapes and that would help her get used to the sound of Italian. When Michael asked why she bought the book and the tapes she explained: 'You can't expect all the locals to speak English and anyway a bit of the language always comes in handy when you're trying to read road signs or make sense of a menu or looking at the label on a bottle of wine'. Michael agreed it was a good idea and said he might try and pick up a word or two himself.

5.4. Word list for critical pronunciations in Dublin English

Apart from the sample sentences, which all informants recorded, and the free text, which many also read (see previous section), there was a third item with which some speakers in Dublin also obliged by allowing themselves to be recorded. This was a list with single words each of which potentially illustrated an item of change in present-day Dublin English. Speakers were asked to read the list slowly.

List of key words with features under investigation

DEAL	MEAL	velarisation of /l/
WHICH	WITCH	loss of voice contrast
MARCH	PARK	retroflexion of /r/
FARE	SQUARE	possible vowel rounding
MILD	WILD	retraction of /aɪ/ (voiced environment)
TIGHT	RIGHT	retraction of /aɪ/ (voiceless environment)
TOY	CHOICE	raising of /ɔɪ/ diphthong
CORK	THOUGHT	raising of back vowels (i)
LOT	BOAT	raising of back vowels (ii)
TOWN	MOUTH	fronting of /aʊ/ onset

6.   Extracts from sound files

6.1.   The structure of file names

In order to facilitate the recognition of recordings and to process them with the supplied software (see Part III *Processing software for atlas data* below) files have been named using a pattern consisting of elements with specific references. By this means users can immediately recognise where the informant in the recording is from, his/her gender, age, etc. Each name is divided as follows.

County identifier	ANT_ (= Antrim), KER_ (= Kerry), MAY_ (= Mayo), etc.
Location	Carlow, Tralee, Westport, etc.
Location size	R2, R1, U2, U1 (ascending order of size)
Gender of informants	_F_ = female, _M_ = male
Age of informant	20, 35, 50, etc. ages are approximate, 'o' means 'over' the age indicated
Recording type	_T = text, _W = words; no reference means the recording consists of the standard set of sentences
Recording number	more than one recording with the same parameters is indicated in brackets, e.g. _(2), _(3), at the end of the name

Examples

1)   MAY_Ballina_R1_M_20_W.wav

Male speaker about 20 from the town of Ballina in Mayo reading a word list.

2)   MAY_Ballina_R1_M_35_T.wav

Male speaker about 35 from the town of Ballina in Mayo reading the free text.

3)   MAY_Westport_R1_F_20_(2).wav

Female speaker about 20 from the town of Westport in Mayo, second recording with identical parameters.

The file names of recordings contain a reference to the size of the location from which speakers came (see third row in table above). The idea behind this is to give a rough idea of whether informants were from a rural or urban location and, if the latter, what the approximate size of this location was. For the purposes of classification a group of four labels were devised as follows.

Label	Location size
R2	below 5,000
R1	between 5,000 and 12,000
U2	between 12,000 and 30,000
U1	over 30,000

One of these labels is to be found in each sound file, except those for the four largest cities in Ireland – Belfast, Derry, Dublin and Cork – all of which obviously belong to the category U1. Bear in mind that Irish towns and cities are rapidly expanding and depending on this growth and the actual lines of urban boundaries, some of the classifications might not be entirely accurate.

6.2. Statistics for sound files

The next table shows the values for the main parameters concerning informant type and background. Some values are determined by external factors, e.g. the large number of recordings for Leinster is due to the fact that this is the province of Ireland with the highest population (its contains Dublin and its environs). The greater number of male informants in the atlas is probably due to the greater readiness of males to do a recording for an adult male stranger. The age spread shows a clear bias towards the region of young adults. This fact is due to a deliberate choice made to compile an atlas which reflects language usage by this segment of present-day Irish society, especially given the changes in pronunciation which have arisen in the last decade or so and which is embodied most clearly in this group. The large number of sentence recordings is simply due to the fact that this was the default reading done by all informants. Only if someone was prepared to do more for the author was a free text recording and/or a word list recording made (the latter only in Dublin).

Files by province	Connaught : 152	Munster : 310	Leinster : 676	Ulster : 379
Location sizes	U1 : 492	U2 : 161	R1 : 424	R2 : 440
Gender spread	Female : 625	Male : 892		
Age spread	under 20 : 71	20 - 30 : 1,225	30 - 50 : 114	Over 50 : 107
Recording type	sentences : 1,194	free text : 186	word list : 137	

6.3. Listening to sound files while reading

The purpose of the following sections is to discuss the salient features of Irish English and indicate the sound files from the atlas where the features in question can be heard. These files are on the DVD and can be accessed by selecting the option *Listen to sound files* in the branch *Sound Atlas – first approach* to be seen in the tree of the Java version of the sound atlas processing software (for details see section III *Processing software for atlas data*, 1.1. *Java version* below). In the right-hand window of the screen a text can be seen entitled *Extracts illustrating salient features of Irish English*. In this text the names of sound files can be seen, the exact same as those given in the following sections. The names here are in typewriter font with the extension .WAV for *wave* file, i.e. sound file. In the Java version of the processing software the names also have the extension .WAV and are highlighted, usually in blue to start with. By clicking on the name of a sound file, you can listen to its contents. When going through the following sections, readers should have the DVD in the drive of their computer and click on the file names to hear the sound files illustrating the features being discussed.

For the ensuing discussions, the sound system of Irish English has been broken down into vowels, consonants and phonological processes. The treatment of consonants is divided into two parts, (i) sonorants and (ii) obstruents and at the end of the section there are remarks on the intonation of Irish English.

As has been mentioned already, there is a clear division between southern and northern Irish English. Because of this there is a special subsection on the salient features of northern Irish English inasmuch as these differ significantly from those of southern Irish English. Although scholars have usually concentrated on one or other of the two main varieties of Irish English, there are nonetheless considerable similarities on all linguistic levels Hickey (1999a), see section 3.6. *Ireland as a linguistic area* above for further details.

6.4. Vowels

Diphthong realisations: (i) AI

As with so many other varieties of English, there is considerable variation in the realisation of the two main rising diphthongs, /ai/ and /au/. The variation in Irish English concerns the onset for both these vowels. With the /ai/ diphthong, it is frequent to find centralisation or a raising and fronting of the onset. The /au/ diphthong, on the other hand, does not show centralisation in Ireland but significant fronting of the onset is found. This is a feature of colloquial speech in the entire east coast of Ireland. Because this is also a feature of local Dublin speech and because more demotic varieties of English in the capital have become accepted in recent years, the fronting of the /au/ diphthong is spreading quite rapidly throughout the entire Republic of Ireland as part of the spread of a supraregional pronunciation.

Centralisation of PRIDE vowel [East Coast]
        DUB_TIME-Centralisation_1.wav
        DUB_TIME-Centralisation_2.wav
        CAR_Carlow_OUTSIDE-Central.wav

No distinction between AI-realisations, voice of environment irrelevant
        CAR_Carlow_PRICE-PRIDE.wav
        LIM_Rathkeale_PRICE-PRIDE.wav
Retracted realisation of AI /_ [+voice], fashionable Dublin English
        DUB_AI-Retraction_1.wav
        DUB_AI-Retraction_2.wav

Retracted realisation of AI in all environments ['Dublin 4'-type accent]
```
    DUB_AI-Dublin4_1.wav
    DUB_AI-Dublin4_2.wav
```

Diphthong realisations: (ii) AU

Lack of AU-fronting in East Coast and South West
```
    CAR_Carlow_AU-NoFronting.wav
    KER_Waterville_AU-NoFront.wav
```

AU-Fronting [Dublin English]
```
    DUB_AU-Fronting_1.wav
    DUB_AU-Fronting_2.wav
```

Diphthong realisations: (iii) OI

The diphthong of the CHOICE lexical set has been subject to considerable raising in recent years (see section 4.1. *English in Dublin* above). Traditionally, the onset of this diphthong has been quite open so that to non-Irish ears the word *boy* sounded like *buy*. Indeed one can interpret the rising of the onset of this diphthong as an unconscious reaction to the more open onset which is typical of conservative varieties of English in Ireland. The raising of the diphthong onset is part of the upward chain shift of low back vowels in present-day Dublin (again see relevant sections above).

Front onset [conservative realisation]
```
    LIM_Rathkeale_CHOICE-Front.wav
```
Raised realisation [new Dublin English]
```
    DUB_Raising-CHOICE.wav
```

Vowel lengthening: (i) the SOFT lexical set

A salient feature of English in the east coast area, and particularly in Dublin, is a long vowel in words of the SOFT lexical set. It can be assumed that this is a conservative feature of Dublin English. Perhaps it does not stem from the original varieties brought the city, but resulted from the superimposition of a longer vowel pronunciation in the early modern period. Certainly the varieties in the southwest and west of the country, which have been most influenced by the shift from Irish (essentially between the 17th and 19th centuries), do not show a long vowel in such words.

Lengthening of vowel in SOFT [Carlow and Dublin speakers]
```
CAR_Carlow_SOFT_VowelLength.wav
DUB_SOFT-LongVowel.wav
```

Lack of vowel lengthening: (i) the SOFT lexical set

Short realisation of SOFT vowel
```
KER_SOFT-ShortVowel.wav
```

Short realisation of SOFT vowel ['Dublin 4'-type accent]
```
DUB_SOFT-ShortVowel-Dublin4.wav
```

Vowel lengthening: (ii) the TRAP lexical set

Conservative supraregional varieties of Irish English do not show a long vowel in the TRAP lexical set. But again in the east coast dialect area – at least in Dublin and the surrounding area – a long vowel is typical here as can be heard in the following sound extract.

Lengthening of low vowels [East Coast feature]
```
CAR_Carlow_TRAP_VowelLength.wav
```

Distinction between DANCE and PATH
```
CAV_Blacklion_DANCE-PATH.wav
```

Short low vowel [South-West pronunciation]
```
KER_TRAP-ShortVowel.wav
```

Lack of vowel lengthening: (ii) the BATH lexical set

East Coast, but not Dublin and environs
```
KIK_Kilkenny_BATH-Short.wav
```

Vowel realisation in the START lexical set

Although Irish English shows a low vowel for the TRAP lexical set, there is one case in which this vowel is considerably raised. This is in the environment before historic /r/ which, as in all cases of Irish English, is pronounced (with the exception of conservative local Dublin English). There are two historic interpretations of this situation. The first is that the raising only occurred in this environment. The second is that the present environment is just a remnant of a much wider distribution characteristic of earlier forms of Irish English. There is a certain amount of evidence that the latter was the case, particularly because prescriptive authors like Thomas Sheridan remarked on the raising of the TRAP vowel to something near the DRESS vowel in late 18th-century Dublin English, specifically not in the environment before /r/.

Local East Coast speaker [older speaker with low central vowel]
    `KIK_Kilkenny_CAR-LowCentral.wav`

North Tipperary speaker [with fronted vowel]
    `TIP_Nenagh_Front-R.wav`

Retracted realisation of vowel in START lexical set ['Dublin 4'-type accent]
    `DUB_START-Dublin4.wav`

Centralisation in the SQUARE lexical set ['Dublin 4'-type accent]

Because an important motive for the Dublin vowel shift has been the dissociation from colloquial varieties of English in the capital, certain features of pronunciation have developed which are diametrically opposed to local features. An example of this is the rounding of the vowel in the SQUARE lexical set. This was found with original 'Dublin 4'-type accents in the 1980s which are, however, now regarded as stuffy and old-fashioned and hence avoided. Non-local Dubliners who grew up in the 1990s do not show this feature.

    `DUB_Centralisation-SQUARE_1.wav`
    `DUB_Centralisation-SQUARE_2.wav`

Distinction between the NURSE and TERM lexical sets

Traditionally forms of Irish English have shown a distinction between the vowels in the TERM and in the NURSE lexical sets (see discussion of these labels in section 5.1. *Lexical sets for Irish English* above). This distinction is maintained both in rural dialects and in popular varieties of English in Dublin.

```
DUB_NURSE-TERM-Distinction.wav
```

Front realisation of vowel in the TERM lexical set
```
LIM_Rathkeale_TERM-MidFront.wav
```

Conservative realisation of vowel in the STRUT lexical set

The realisation of the vowel in the STRUT lexical set is always different from southern British English. The supraregional realisation is quite retracted and somewhat rounded when compared to that in RP. This realisation resembles, if it is not identical to, the realisation of a similar vowel in Irish.

```
SLI_Easky_CUT.wav
```

High back realisation of vowel in the STRUT lexical set

The only variety of Irish English which shows a back rounded high vowel for the STRUT lexical set is popular Dublin English. This realisation is a common stereotype, particularly as the vowel occurs in the first syllable of the city's name. There is no doubt that this is a conservative feature of Dublin English which in this respect was not influenced by forms of Irish English which were shaped by the shift from Irish to English in the early modern period. These latter varieties used a vowel from Irish which is very similar acoustically to that of the STRUT realisation in present-day Irish English (see the discussion in Hickey 1986b), e.g. Irish *doras* [dʌrəs] 'door', *fliuch* [fʲlʲʌx] 'wet'. This lowered variant made its way into the supraregional variety of English in the south of Ireland and has remained there since. The precise route this [ʌ] vowel took is uncertain but one view worth considering is that it was adopted into late 19th century mainstream Dublin English as an alternative to the local [ʊ] vowel. An influence in Dublin of speakers from rural parts of Ireland, typically the west and south-west, can be posited given that the rise in population of some 10% during the second half of the 19th century was due to in-migration from rural areas. The [ʌ] vowel had an inherent advantage for middle-class speakers in Dublin

– and hence in the rest of Ireland through supraregionalisation – because it provided them with a means of dissociating themselves from local speakers in the STRUT lexical set.

```
DUB_STRUT-HighBackVowel.wav
```

For similar argumentation with regard to the THINK and BREATHE lexical sets, see section *Alveolar realisations of THINK and BREATHE lexical sets* below.

The GOAT lexical set

In conservative rural varieties of Irish English this vowel is realised as a monophthong, i.e. [oː]. Up to the present supraregional varieties have had a slightly diphthongised realisation, i.e. [ou]. Fashionable varieties of Dublin English show more strongly diphthongised realisations with a vowel like [əu]. Local varieties of Dublin English on the other hand are characterised by a low starting point, yielding [ʌo]. This pronunciation is avoided in all supraregional varieties. For the purposes of disassociation within Dublin it might be imagined that the monophthong would be sufficient. However, this is regarded as an old-fashioned country pronunciation nowadays. The solution for non-local speakers of Dublin English has been to adopt the strongly diphthongised pronunciation which is quite similar to that found in southern British English. There may also have been pressure in vowel space for the further diphthongisation of the GOAT vowel. Given that the vowel in the THOUGHT lexical set has been raised considerably in new Dublin English (see section 4.1. *English in Dublin* above), one could posit that this would lead to congestion in mid back vowel space and so the further diphthongisation of [ou] to [əu] was undertaken to avoid this, the centralisation of the diphthong onset to [ə] providing additional acoustic separation from the raised [oː] in *thought* [t̠oːt̠].

The local pronunciation of the GOAT lexical set, which has an onset in the region of [ʌ], is probably of considerable vintage because it is found nowhere else in Ireland.

Monophthong [conservative rural speakers]
```
KER_Kenmare_GOAT-Monophth.wav
KER_Waterville_GOAT-Monoph.wav
```

Diphthong [fashionable Dublin English]
```
DUB_GOAT-Diphthong_1.wav
DUB_GOAT-Diphthong_2.wav
```

In the following sound file, four speakers are to be heard. The first is a local Dubliner with *goat* [gʌoh], the second is a mainstream speaker with *go* [goː], the third is a female in her thirties with *go* [gou] while the last is a female around 20 with the advanced realisation *goat* [gəʊt̪].

Four realisations of the GOAT lexical set [Dublin English]
```
DUB_FourGOATrealisations.wav
```

The FACE lexical set

The realisation of the FACE lexical set is not of any sociolinguistic relevance in the south of Ireland and is usually a monophthong. In Dublin speech there may be a very slight tendency to have a diphthong with a lower starting point.

```
LIM_Rathkeale_FACE-Monophth.wav
```

The NORTH lexical set

In conservative forms of Irish English, both local and supraregional, there has always been a clear acoustic distinction between the vowel in the NORTH set and a vowel in the FORCE set. The latter has always shown [oː] and continues to do so whereas the former set has had a relatively open vowel. In recent forms of Irish English emanating from younger generation speakers in Dublin the vowel in the NORTH set is considerably raised, leading in most cases to homophony with FORCE.
Open realisation
```
KER_Waterville_NORTH-Open.wav
KIK_Kilkenny_NORTH-VeryOpen.wav
```

Contrast between NORTH and FORCE [*morning* ~ *mourning* distinction]
```
KIK_Kilkenny_NORTH-FORCE.wav
```

Open realisation [with non-rhotic vowel]
```
LIM_Rathkeale_ALL-OpenVowel.wav
```

Tense unstressed high front vowel [HAPPY-tensing]

The final vowel in the word HAPPY is always pronounced tense so that the issue of HAPPY-tensing, so much discussed in literature on the phonology of British English, is of no relevance in Ireland. The only exception to this is varieties of northern Irish English which show general lowering of the short front vowels of the KIT and DRESS lexical sets. Such varieties show [ɪ] or [e] in the HAPPY set (see section 6.4.1. *Specific features of northern Irish English* below).

```
KIK_Kilkenny_HAPPY-Tensing.wav
```

Breaking of high front vowels [local Dublin English]

A feature of long vowel realisation in local Dublin English is that there tends to be a breaking of these vowels. This is realised by [j] with [iː] and by [w] with [uː]. This breaking is regarded as a stereotypical feature and is clearly avoided by all speakers of non-local Dublin English.

```
DUB_Long_I-Breaking_1.wav
DUB_Long_I-Breaking_2.wav
```

6.4.1. Specific features of northern Irish English

Northern vowel fronting

One of the most prominent features of English in the north of Ireland is the fronting of the vowel in the GOOSE lexical set, i.e. [gʉs]. This is a realisation which is shared with varieties of English in Scotland. Indeed Scotland and Northern Ireland can in this respect be regarded as a linguistic area because the fronting is also found in Irish and in Scottish Gaelic. The fronting of the GOOSE vowel also affects the realisation of the /au/ diphthong, i.e. the words in the MOUTH lexical set have an [ʉ] endpoint.

Fronting of GOOSE vowel
```
    DER_U-Fronting.wav
```

Fronting of endpoint in AU-diphthong
        CAV_Blacklion_AU-fronting.wav

Lowering of the KIT vowel

Another salient feature of northern Irish English is the lowering of short front vowels. This affects the vowel of the KIT lexical set in particular.

        ANT_KIT-VowelLowering.wav

Retraction of the TRAP vowel when preceding labials

The vowel in the TRAP lexical set can vary considerably in northern Irish English. This vowel tends to be fronted when it occurs before velars and retracted when found before labials.

        ANT_TRAP-VowelRetraction.wav

Palatalisation of velars when preceding the TRAP vowel

An almost stereotypical feature of northern Irish English is the palatalisation of velars before vowels of the TRAP lexical set. This is probably a feature of early modern English which has been retained in the north of Ireland but is generally lost in British English. The feature was also transported to the Caribbean area (Harris 1986).

        ANT_VelarPalatalisation.wav

Breaking of vowel in the FACE lexical set

Although the pronunciation of the FACE lexical set varies little and is not sociolinguistically relevant in the south of Ireland it does show a distinctive realisation in the north. Here the vowel is diphthongised with a schwa offglide.

        ANT_FACE-VowelBreaking.wav

Tensed and raised realisation of the AI-diphthong

In northern Irish English the onset of the vowel in the PRICE lexical set is considerably raised compared to varieties of English in the south of the country.

```
ANT_AI-TensedRealisation.wav
```

Flap realisation of intervocalic T

A flap realisation of intervocalic /-t-/ is to be found widely in Northern Ireland. It is also – unrelatedly – a feature of recent supraregional southern Irish English.

```
ANT_T-IntervocalicTap.wav
```

Deletion in intervocalic DH

The intervocalic realisation of DH /ð/ varies across Northern Ireland. In conservative varieties, which are closely linked to Ulster Scots, this sound tends to be deleted. In forms of Derry English the sound can be realised as /l/.

```
ANT_DH-IntervocalicDeletion.wav
```

Lack of phonemic vowel length in Ulster Scots

In common with many forms of English in Scotland, northern Irish English, particularly that of Scots origin, does not show a phonemic distinction in vowel length.

```
ANT_LackOfDistVowelLength.wav
```

Shift of DH to L in Derry English [ongoing change]

The shift illustrated by the current sound file appears to be of quite recent origin and may well have a distribution determined by ethnic community in west Ulster, specifically in the city of Derry, see McCafferty (1999, 2001) for detailed discussions. Here the Catholic community seem to be leading the shift of intervocalic /ð/ to /l/.

```
DER_DH-L-Shift.wav
```

6.5.   Sonorants and approximants

6.5.1.   *Realisations of /l/*

Traditionally, Irish English is known for an alveolar realisation of /l/. The general assumption is that speakers of Irish chose the clear /l/ of their native language as the closest equivalent to the lateral in the forms of English they were exposed to. This assumption is corroborated by observations among native speakers of Irish who use an alveolar [l] in most positions and the velarised [ɫ] of Irish occasionally, particularly before the diphthong /ai/ as in *like* [ɫaɪk].

However, more recent supraregional varieties of English in the south of Ireland all show a clearly velarised /l/ in syllable-final position. In all likelihood the origin of this is local Dublin English. It would appear that more general varieties of English in the capital adopted this pronunciation of /l/. The only other variety of English in Ireland where velarised [ɫ] occurs widely is Ulster Scots (where it has frequently being vocalised) and there is no question of this having had an influence on supraregional varieties of English in the Republic of Ireland. The adoption of a velarised [ɫ] has meant that the acoustic distance between new supraregional varieties and older conservative varieties has been increased.

Alveolar [l]
    CAR_Carlow_Alveolar-L.wav
    KER_Kenmare_Alveolar-L.wav

Velarised [l]
    DUB_Velarised-L_1.wav
    DUB_Velarised-L_2.wav

6.5.2.   *Realisations of /r/*

All forms of Irish English are rhotic. The only exception to this is conservative popular Dublin English. However, this exception is particularly important when considering the evolution of supraregional varieties of Irish English. When one bears in mind that the development of new Dublin English in the past decade or so has been characterised by the dissociation from more local varieties of English in the city, then one can understand why a retroflex [ɻ] should have arisen and why it has been picked up so readily by the younger generation in present-day Ireland. The point to grasp about the retroflex [ɻ] is that it is quite different from the weak [ɹ] of local Dublin English. This relationship can be viewed in terms of a cline of rhoticity: at one end there is local Dublin English with very low or non-existent rhoticity, at the other end one has new varieties of Dublin English which show a very clear retroflex [ɻ]. There is a clear acoustic difference between a local pronunciation like [fæːˠm] and a fashionable pronunciation like [fæˑˈɻm]. The [ɪ] onglide to the retroflex [ɻ] increases the acoustic perception of rhoticity.

Low rhoticity of local Dublin English
        DUB_LowRhoticity-local.wav

High rhoticity of new Dublin English
        DUB_HighRhoticity-fashion.wav

This retroflex /r/ has spread throughout the country because of the influence of non-local Dublin speech. The adoption by the younger generation, particularly by females, may well have been strengthened by the fact that this type of pronunciation is distinctly non-Irish (but will become so by use, of course). Hence it is, in terms of their perception, 'cool'.

The traditional realisation of post-vocalic /r/ is a non-retroflex continuant, usually with a degree of velarisation, i.e. [ɹ] or [ɫ]. This does not have the [ɪ]-onglide of the retroflex /r/.

Traditional realisation of post-vocalic /r/ [non-retroflex]
        CAR_Carlow_SORE-NonRetroflx.wav
        KER_Kenmare_SORE-NonRetrofl.wav

A further twist to the question of /r/ realisation in Ireland can be found. There is a strong body of evidence for a uvular [ʁ] along the east coast. There are many reports of this type of /r/ being used particularly in the southeast of the country, for example, it is supposed to have been typical of rural pronunciations in Co. Waterford. However, the clearest remnants of this type of pronunciation are to be found in the north of the province Leinster, in an area from Drogheda up to Dundalk and along the south side of the present-day border with Northern Ireland. There can be little doubt that this uvular [ʁ] is a relic of the first form of English in the east coast of Ireland and has been replaced (i) by an alveolar [ɹ] in the south of Ireland and (ii) by a retroflex [ɻ] typical of varieties of northern Irish English encroaching downwards into north Leinster.

This fact is of interest for the typology of English dialects. Hitherto a uvular [ʁ] was thought only to occur in Northumbria in the north-east of England as the so-called Northumbrian 'burr'. This finding in the recordings of the sound atlas also helps to explain the origin of the uvular [ʁ] found in isolated pockets in Newfoundland. It could well have been transported there by emigrants from the east coast of Ireland.

Uvular [ʁ] with North Leinster speaker
        LOU_Drogheda_Uvular_R.wav

The uvular [ʁ] extends across north Leinster under the border with the north and is found in Cavan, for instance with the speaker from Blacklion [north-west Cavan] in the following sound files.

Uvular [ʁ] with from area bordering with north
        CAV_Blacklion_Uvularisation.wav

6.5.3. Approximants

Like other conservative forms of English in the British Isles, Irish English traditionally used a voiceless labio-velar approximant in all words which are written with an initial *wh-*. This has meant that there was a phonetic contrast between such words and those beginning with *w-* which could – and still can with older speakers – be heard as a distinction in voice. This distinction would appear to be receding presently and if newer forms of Dublin English are anything to go by, then the distinction will die out quite shortly as it is not maintained by younger speakers of Irish English.

Voiceless labio-velar approximant in WHICH lexical set
        KER_Waterville_WHICH.wav

```
SLI_Easky_WHICH.wav
```

Voiced labio-velar approximant in WHICH lexical set
```
DUB_WHICH-WITCH-NoDistinct.wav
```

6.6. Obstruents [stops and fricatives]

Fricative realisation of T in the WET lexical set

The fricative realisation of /t/ is a prominent feature of southern Irish English. It has been described in various manners, 'fricative *t*' or 'slit *t*' being the most common labels. By this is meant that /t/ in positions of high sonority, e.g. at the end of words and before a pause or intervocalically, is realised as a sound with all the attributes of /t/ but a fricative, i.e. as an apico-alveolar fricative (Hickey 1984). It is not an affricate and not an /s/-sound, these descriptions stem from non-Irish scholars who have not observed the sounds accurately.

The fricative realisation of /t/ has not been the subject of sociolinguistic censure and for this reason there has been no movement away from it in recent forms of Irish English. Perhaps the only exception to this is the use of a flap as the realisation of /t/ in intervocalic position.

```
KIK_Kilkenny_T-Frication.wav
DUB_T-Frication.wav
```

Realisation of medial T as flap [new Dublin English]

```
DUB_T-IntervocalicFlap.wav
```

Realisation of medial T as H [local Dublin English]

The lenition of *t*, to be seen in the 'fricative *t*' just described, is part of a cline which reaches through /h/ and a glottal stop to zero. The realisation as /h/ is found in supraregional varieties in the word *Saturday*, possibly due to the former influence of Irish *Sahairn* with intervocalic /-h-/. Local forms of Dublin English are characterised by a realisation of *t* as either *h* or zero. It frequently occurs as a glottal stop in word-final position.

```
DUB_MedialT-to-H.wav
```

Glottalisation of T in word-final position [local Dublin English]

    DUB_T-GlottalStopRealisat.wav

Deletion of T in final position [local Dublin English]

    DUB_Final-T-Deletion.wav

Distinction between dental and alveolar stops

In virtually all forms of southern Irish English the sounds in the lexical sets THINK and BREATHE are realised as stops. However, a spelling pronunciation with a final fricative is common in a reading style and is found in many recordings of the sound atlas. The stop realisation, like the fricative one, is dental. Because of this, a distinction between dental and alveolar stops has arisen in Irish English. This is an acoustic difference which the non-Irish are not always good at recognising, let alone practising themselves. It can be heard clearly on the files of the sound atlas, for instance, in the following sample.

    DUB_DentalAlveolarDistinct.wav

Alveolar realisations of THINK and BREATHE lexical sets

In traditional rural of varieties of Irish English, especially in the east, south and southwest of the country, the THINK and BREATHE lexical sets are realised with alveolar stops. However, this is not true of the west of the country which shows dental realisations. In the north of the country one finds fricatives in these lexical sets.

In supraregional varieties of English in the Republic of Ireland the THINK and BREATHE lexical sets show dental realisations. Given the fact that the supraregional variety of southern Irish English had its origin in middle-class Dublin usage and that in local Dublin English the THINK and BREATHE lexical sets show alveolar realisations, the question arises as to where the dental realisations came from. One explanation, put forward by the present author, is that the dental realisation was adopted from migrants from the west of Ireland moving to Dublin in the latter half of the 19th century. There was considerable influx from rural regions of the west of Ireland to the Dublin area in search of work or on their way to emigrate abroad. These speakers would have had a dental realisation for the THINK and BREATHE lexical sets because they would have substituted the realisation in their varieties of the Irish language for the /θ/ and /ð/ sounds in the sets in question. There were two inherent advantages in adopting the pronunciation of the western rural speakers: (1) it furthered dissociation from speakers of local Dublin English and (2) it 'demerged' the words of the THINK and TWO lexical sets so that pairs like *tinker* and *thinker* were no longer homophonous.

Alveolarisation of stop in BREATHE lexical set
```
CAV_Blacklion_DH-Alveolar.wav
```

Alveolarisation of stop in THINK lexical set
```
SLI_Easky_TH-Alveolarisat.wav
```

Dentalisation of T

In vernacular forms of Irish English, particularly in the north of the country, the realisation of /t/ before /r/ can be dental, i.e. [t̪ɹ-]. This realisation has a long tradition in Ireland and is generally indicated in eye dialect as *thr-* or *dhr-*.

```
SLI_Easky_T-Dentalisation.wav
```

6.7. Phonological processes

Metathesis and epenthesis

Both metathesis and epenthesis are areal phenomena in Ireland (Hickey 1999a). They occur with a wide scope in Irish and also in English where they are frequent in more vernacular forms of the language. In supraregional forms of Irish English the main clusters to be affected by metathesis are those consisting of a short vowel and /r/ as in *pattern* ['pætɹən]. More local forms of English show metathesis in clusters consisting /s/ and /p/ as in *hospital* [hɑstɪpəl]. Other instances, such as *ask* [æks], no longer appear to be attested but are documented abundantly for earlier forms of Irish English.

Metathesis in sequences of V + /r/
```
WEX_Enniscorthy_R-Vowel-Metath.wav
```

Epenthesis is clearly in evidence in the Irish English pronunciation of the word *film* as ['fɪləm]. This applies across the entire country. Epenthesis in clusters of /-rm/ or /-rn/ is less common, though the pronunciation *farm* ['fæːɹəm] is amply attested in the sound atlas. The phonological reason for epenthesis lies in a prohibition on heavy clusters in Irish English. The sonorants which comprise such clusters are resyllabified by the introduction of an epenthetic schwa between them.

Epenthesis in L-M-sequences [South-West speaker]
    KER_Kenmare_LM-Epethesis.wav

Epenthesis in L-M-sequences [young Dublin English speaker]
    DUB_L-M-Epenthesis.wav

Epenthesis in R-M-sequences
    LIM_Rathkeale_RM-Epenthesis.wav

Epenthesis in R-N-sequences
    CAR_Carlow_RN-Epen-Meta.wav

Plosivisation of /s/

A feature of the southeast of Ireland, and apparently stretching into the south as well, is the plosivisation of /s/, something which is widely attested for vernacular forms of English in the southern United States. It is particularly common with grammatical words, for instance in negative forms of *be*, as in *isn't* [ɪdn̩t].

    KER_Kenmare_S-Plosivation.wav

Yod deletion

In Irish English there is widespread deletion of yod in a position follow-ing an alveolar sonorant in stressed position, e.g. *news* [nuːz]. This dele-tion does not apply after obstruents, e.g. *stew* is [stjuː]. Nor does the deletion apply after labials or in unstressed position, e.g. the yod is maintained in words like *mews* and *numerical*.

    LIM_Rathkeale_NEW-YodDelet.wav

Nasal alveolarisation

The common shift of [ŋ] to [n] in unstressed position, above all in the continuous form of verbs, is widespread in the whole of Ireland. In the north there would seem to be a greater tolerance of this shift in non-local speech.

```
LIM_Rathkeale_NG-Alveolar.wav
```

6.8. Intonation and stress patterns

Typical intonation for the South-West of Ireland

There are two respects in which the South-West of Ireland can be regarded as a separate dialect area. The first involves the raising of [ɛ] to [ɪ] before nasals as in *again* [əgɪn] (this raising used to be much more widespread in Irish English and has been maintained longest in the South-West).

The second unique feature of the South-West is the distinctive sentence intonation which applies west of Co. Waterford, encompassing the entire counties of Cork and Kerry. A distinctive feature of this intonation is the fall-rise melody to be found in stressed syllables containing long vowels.

```
KER_Kenmare_Intonation.wav
KER_Waterville_Intonation.wav
```

Stress attraction by heavy syllables late in word

There are a large number of verbs in English which consist of three syllables, the last of which is heavy, e.g. *educate, realise, contemplate, distribute.* Such words provide a prosodic pattern in which stress is attracted to the final heavy syllable. There have been various views on why this stress pattern should be typical of Irish English. Some scholars, such as Alan Bliss, believe that the stress pattern of southern dialects of Irish may have provided a model, as these show stress on heavy non-initial syllables. But there is sufficient variation in stress patterning in mainland British English so that one does not have to assume Irish influence here.

```
TIP_Nenagh_StressAttraction.wav
```

III Processing software for atlas data

1. A Sound Atlas of Irish English

The DVD accompanying this book contains all the sound files, maps, images, textual data and software of the sound atlas. There are essentially two ways of listening to the sound files and accessing the additional data:

1) By availing of the Java version of the sound atlas which is to be found on the DVD.
2) By installing the Windows software which is also to be found on the DVD and then launching this software from your hard disk.

In both cases you can access all the sound files and most of the additional data, although there are a few restrictions with the Java version. It is recommended that you start with the Java version as this will run on all types of computers and under the various operating systems which are current today. Furthermore, it requires no installation.

1.1. Java version

The Java version of the sound atlas utilises the technology of internet browsers and their various components to display data of various types. To start the Java version of the sound atlas, proceed as follows (on a PC): start the Windows *Explorer*, then log onto the DVD. Double click on this file (the first in the root directory): `000_Sound_Atlas.htm`. On an Apple *Macintosh* the name of this file will appear on the desktop once you insert the DVD into the drive of the computer and you can then open this file. In both cases the operating system of the computer (PC or *Macintosh*) will use the default browser to load the Java version of the sound atlas. Users of *Macintosh* computers should note that the supplied browser *Safari* produced slightly better results than the *Internet Explorer* during many tests on Apple computers made by the author.

When the sound atlas begins it will present you with an Explorer-like tree containing several branches and nodes.

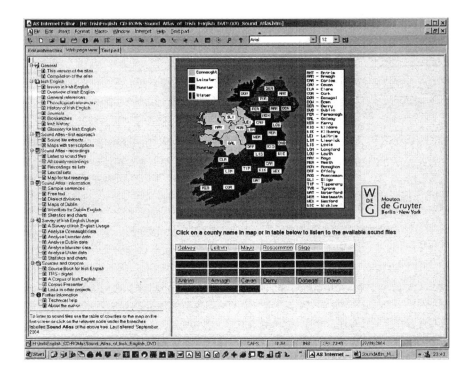

Each node is associated with an element of the sound atlas. All you need to do is click on a node to access the information associated with it. To listen to the sound files you must have a soundcard in your computer with loudspeakers or headphones attached. The operating system of your computer will then use the default software module to play the sound files. On a PC this may well be the Windows *Media Player* and on a *Macintosh* this is likely to be *Apple Quick Time*.

Once the Java version starts you can immediately access the recordings of the sound atlas. This can be done by clicking on the name of a county in the table with county names or by clicking on a county label in the map of Ireland, both on the right-hand side of the screen. A popup window opens as can be seen below.

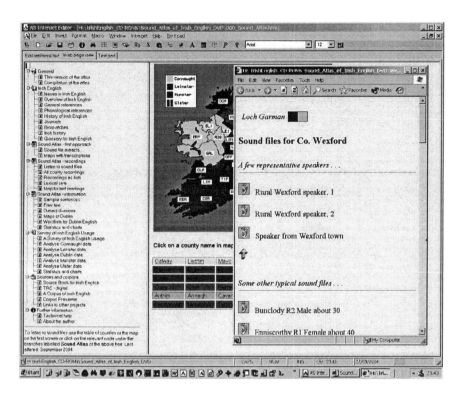

In this window (the layout is the same for all counties) you will notice that there are three groups of data.

1)   A few representative speakers
2)   Some other typical sound files
3)   All sound files for this county

The idea here is to provide an increasingly detailed acoustic picture of Irish English for the county in question. The division of the country by county is deliberate as Ireland is arranged into administrative units which are large enough to be taken as areas of characteristic speech. However, it should be borne in mind that many features apply across counties, though few vary within a single county. The counties of Ireland also vary in size. Counties like Cork, Kerry, Galway, Mayo, Tipperary, Donegal are considerably larger than others such as Carlow, Sligo or

Louth (the smallest in the country). For this reason the number of recordings for each county varies. Furthermore, the presence of a large city determines the number of sound files. Counties such as Dublin, Antrim (with Belfast), Derry, Cork, Galway, Waterford, Limerick all have cities of appreciable size for which a representative number of speaker recordings are available.

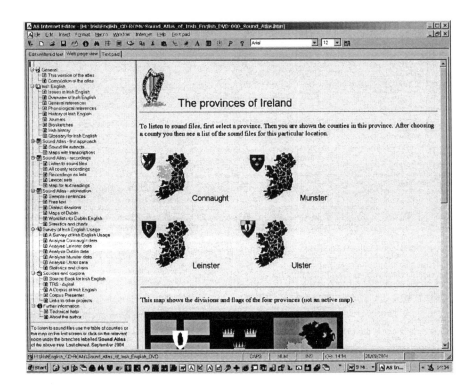

The recordings of the sound atlas can also be accessed by proceeding to the branch labelled *Sound atlas – recordings* in the tree on the left-hand side of the screen. The first node of this branch, *Listen to sound files*, will lead to four small maps of Ireland being displayed in which a single province is highlighted.

By clicking on a map a list of all the counties in the province is shown. The number of counties varies for each province, for instance there are nine in Ulster (six of which form the state of Northern Ireland). By clicking on the name of a county its map appears showing the locations from which speakers were recorded for the sound atlas. A popup window will appear when you click on the county map. In this window the sound files for the particular county are listed. This is the same popup as is available from the screen displayed initially when the Java version of the sound atlas is loaded.

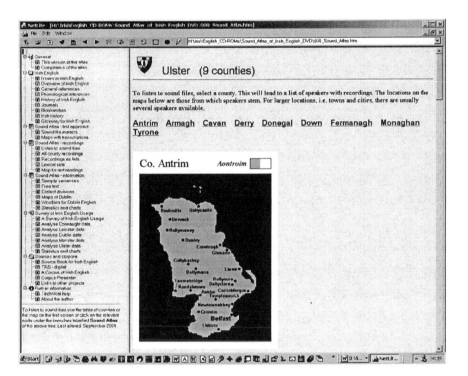

1.1.1. Statistics for the sound atlas

In all, there are a total of 1,517 sound files in the sound atlas. These consist of informants reading out the sample sentences which embody the lexical sets of relevance to Irish English along with a number of free text readings and in addition a certain percentage of Dublin informants reading a short word list in which pronunciations of relevance to linguistic change in present-day Dublin English were captured.

As all informants read the sample sentences, the number of recordings of these equals the number of unique speakers in the sound atlas, i.e. 1,194 individuals. The list in the following screenshot indicates the statistics for this group. The second list (not visible here for reasons of space) indicates the numerical spread for all three types of recordings.

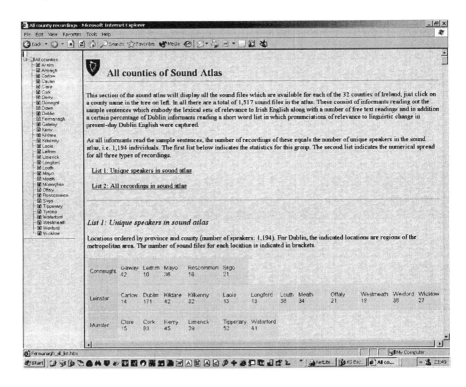

There is a section of the Java atlas software (the last option in the branch *Sound Atlas – information*) which offers various statistics for different parameters of the sound atlas recordings. These are presented both in the form of tables and of charts. To view a chart just click on the relevant button in the centre of the screen. The chart which is displayed can be copied – for instance into your word processor – by selecting it (drag the mouse while pressing the left button) and then copying it via Ctrl-C or the relevant option in the small menu which appears on clicking the right mouse button.

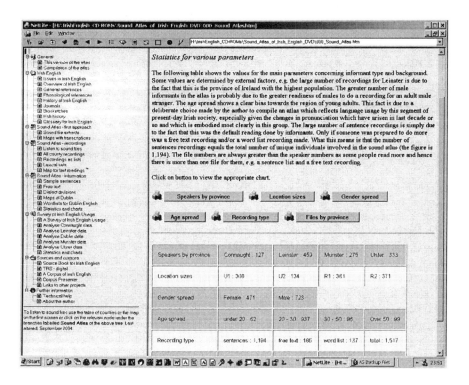

1.1.2. Lexical sets in the sound atlas

As explained in section 5.1. *Lexical sets for Irish English* above, the sample sentences which all speakers were requested to read for a recording were devised to illustrate the lexical sets which are necessary for Irish English. There are two nodes in the sound atlas tree at which the realisations of these lexical sets can be heard. The first consists of a module which offers a series of sound files illustrating the main pronunciations of five major varieties of Irish English (the second node is more detailed, see below). At the top of the module the lexical sets are listed and by clicking on any one of these the map associated with this set is displayed. On the map there are five boxes corresponding to the varieties for which there are sound files (click on the relevant box to listen to the pronunciation). The sound files are accompanied by phonetic transcriptions of key features on the maps. By concentrating on a small number of varieties and by offering transcriptions of the key sounds of 35 lexical sets it is hoped that those new to *A Sound Atlas of Irish English* – above all students – will find it easy to orientate themselves in the arena of Irish English varieties.

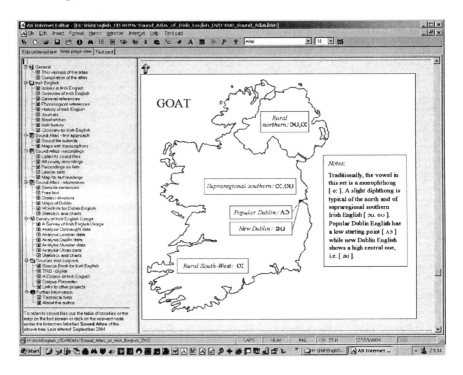

The varieties selected here illustrate different kinds of English in Ireland. The five chosen exemplify the following main regions:

Variety chosen	Illustrating
1) Rural northern	Scots-based speech in Ulster
2) Supraregional southern	Broad-based non-vernacular variety in the south of Ireland
3) Popular Dublin	Vernacular usage in the southern capital
4) New Dublin	Pronunciation which arose in Dublin in the late 1990s
5) Rural South-West	Rural vernacular typical of an area far removed from urban speech of the east

The phonetic symbols used on the active maps of this module are based a broad transcription in which details are not represented. Some of these would have been problematic anyway as many subtleties of pronunciation are difficult to represent phonetically. For instance, the sample phrase for the BREA<u>THE</u> lexical set is *Now breathe in slowly please*. The vowel in the final word would be transcribed /iː/ making the realisation the same for both the local Dublin speaker and the one with the newer pronunciation. Speakers of Irish English would, however, have little doubt in telling the two apart by just this one word, *please*. The reason is probably that the vowel for the local speaker has slight diphthongisation which sets it off from that of the speaker with the new Dublin accent. It is very much a question of transcriptional style whether one indicates such minute differences in pronunciation with different symbols.

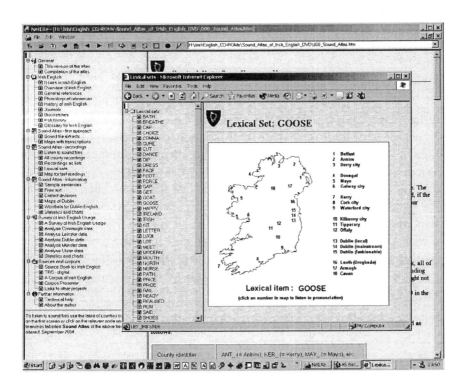

Variation in pronunciation – with one and the same speaker – is another issue which one is confronted with when compiling a sound atlas. For instance, the key sound of the THINK lexical set may well be a fricative in final position, i.e. in a word like *path*. This is due to the relative weakness of syllable-final position (possibly aided by the knowledge that this sound is a fricative in English spoken outside of Ireland and hence used in the normative context of reading which contrasts with spontaneous speech).

More detailed examples of lexical set realisations can be found under the node *Lexical sets* in the branch *Sound Atlas - recordings* in the tree on the left. On first selecting this node a window opens and an explanatory text can be seen in which the vocalic and consonantal lexical sets are displayed and commented on. The sample sentences which embody these lexical sets and which were read aloud by all speakers can also be viewed. In the lexical set window there is also a tree, this time with all the lexical sets for which there are recordings in the sound atlas.

1.1.3. Listening to selected sound files

In the branch *Sound Atlas – first approach* there is a further node labelled *Selection of sound files* which presents a selection from all the sound files in the form of a hierarchical tree. This option is similar to that in the Windows software (see below) and shows approximately one fifth of all the full recordings from the sound atlas. The files have been chosen by the author as representative of the various counties. As with the popup window which appears when an item in the county list in the opening screen is clicked, each county branch in the current tree offers a few typical speakers to begin with and a further node entitle *More files...* through which a further (slightly larger) group of representative files can be accessed.

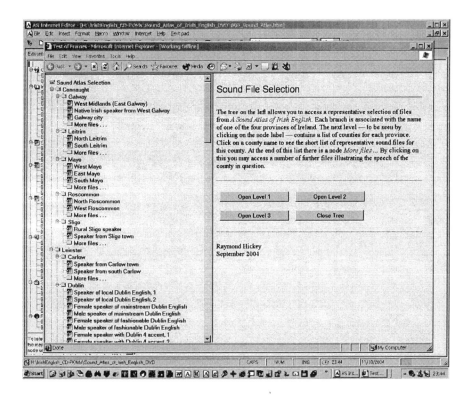

1.1.4. Additional material

There is additional material in this version of the sound atlas which can be accessed through various further nodes of the tree. For instance, information on the dialect divisions in Ireland can be found. There are other maps which provide more detailed information where necessary. A case in point is Dublin for which there are several hundred recordings in the sound atlas, representing the different parts of the city with speakers of different ages and genders.

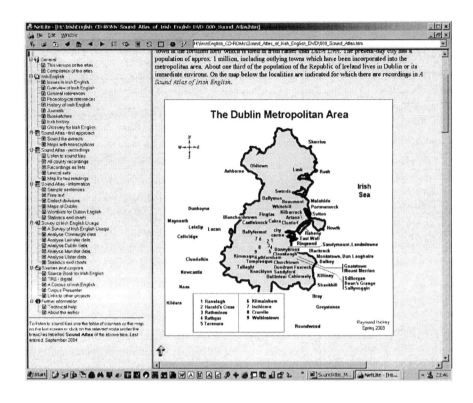

1.1.5. Using other processing software

A further option regarding the data files on the DVD concerns the user's choice of processing software. None of the data is encrypted or in any way restricted to being processed by the supplied software. The different kinds of data are available in the following file formats.

Data type	File format
Text files	Rich Text Format (RTF) files Text (TXT) files
Images and maps	JPG, GIF and BMP files
Sound files	Wave (WAV) files in MP3 format

Users can process these files with their preferred software if they wish. All the data files are to be found below a subdirectory on the DVD (and on the hard disk if installed to a computer) which is labelled \SAIE_Data. For instance, users may wish to use audio processing software with the sound files. This could be beneficial when listening to acoustic details in the recordings (there are many commercial software packages which allow the display of sound files in wave form).

There are a small number of other file types which are used by the supplied software, e.g. list (LST) files and initialisation (INI) files. These are not intended for direct processing by users and should not be tampered with.

Bear in mind that users are legally required to acknowledge the source of data, including extracts from files, which they may use for their own purposes, such as for academic research and publication.

1.2. Windows version

On the DVD there is also a version of the processing software designed for use under Windows on an Intel-based personal computer. To install the supplied Windows software to your computer, start the Windows *Explorer*, double click on setup.exe in the root directory of the DVD and follow the instructions of the installation procedure (steps 1 and 2). During step 1 you will be asked if you wish to copy the sound files to your hard disk as well. If you say 'yes' you will need 3.2 GB (3,200 MB) of free disk space, if you answer 'no' when prompted then you only require 160 MB of space. When the installation is complete there will be a folder entitled *A Sound Atlas of Irish English* on the desktop of your computer. Within this folder there are a number of programmes, the main one of which is also called *A Sound Atlas of Irish English*. Double click on its icon (a loudspeaker on a blue background) and the programme SAIE.exe will start. Now you can choose to examine all the sound files of the sound atlas, only a selection of these or choose one of several other options. If you have not copied the sound files onto your hard disk during installation you must leave the DVD in its drive and select the file SAIE_Selection.dts (for approximately one fifth of the files) or SoundAtlasIrishEnglish.dts (for all files) when you choose to listen to recordings. Both the .dts files are to be found in the directory \SAIE_Data on the DVD. If you copy the sound files to your hard disk then the data set files just referred to will be found in the directory `C:\Program Files\A Sound Atlas of Irish English\ SAIE_Data`. The beginning of this path may be different if you install the software to another location other than `C:` and/or if you are running a non-English version of Windows in which case `Program Files` with be labelled differently, e.g. `Programme` in the German version of Windows.

1.2.1. Main programme

The software package on the accompanying DVD contains a number of programmes for processing the data of the sound atlas. The main programme in this group is itself called *A Sound Atlas of Irish English* and has the name `SAIE.exe` for the operating system. During the process of installing the contents of the DVD this programme and others are copied with all the data to the hard disk of your computer (if you choose to install the sound files as well). As mentioned above, after installation there will be a folder on the Windows desktop of your computer called *A Sound Atlas of Irish English*. Within this folder the present programme is to be found. It offers an interface to all the data files of the sound atlas. The purpose of the programme is to facilitate quick orientation within the varieties of Irish English. The operation of the programme is quite straightforward and many of the options are those you would expect from a programme running in the Windows environment. The easiest way to get to know what data can be accessed is to start the option *All choices*. This can be reached via the *File* menu on the top left-hand side of the screen or can be loaded by pressing Control-A or by clicking on the icon in the toolbar on the second top line of the screen. There are now a set of seven options at your disposal.

The first option offers an introduction to Irish English. It provides historical information, traces the rise of key features of Irish English and discusses the present-day situation in some detail. Of particular importance is the dialectal diversity in the country, specifically the division between a northern and a southern type of pronunciation.

When you begin to listen to the sound files you will notice that most speakers are young people. This fact reflects a conscious decision made by the author at the outset. The broad intention of the current survey is to offer an overview of what contemporary Irish English is like and in what direction it is presently evolving. For this goal the speech of the younger generation is of special significance for it is this social group which is setting the stage for the future development of English, both in the north and the south of the country. Furthermore, it is their speech which will represent the future supraregional varieties within both Northern Ireland and the Republic of Ireland. For the Republic, there is firm evidence that the pronunciation of young, non-local Dubliners is spreading rapidly throughout the entire country (see section 4.1.3. *The spread of the new Dublin accent* above).

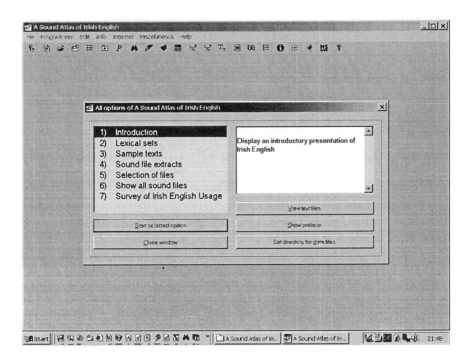

In order to document the pronunciation found in different forms of Irish English a procedure has been adopted which is now common practice in variety studies. This is to use lexical sets (Wells 1982) to illustrate the pronunciation of whole groups of words within a variety (see detailed explanation above). Among the options in the *All choices* menu there is one labelled *Lexical sets*. On activating this a window opens in which there is a list of keywords on the left and an outline map of Ireland on the right.

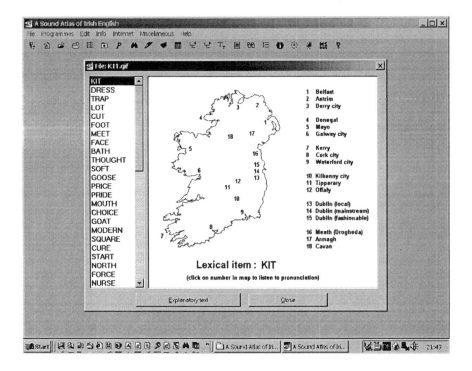

On this map there are locations indicated by numbers. If you click on a number you hear a representative speaker from this region speaking a short sentence which contains the lexical set keyword selected in the list on the left. By this means you can check easily on a whole series of pronunciations throughout Ireland, both north and south. You can also choose to view an explanatory text which explains the principle of lexical sets and discusses some of the particular adaptations which have been necessary for the investigation of Irish English.

The third option will display an active map which you can use to listen to any of a selection of sample texts. The map has numbers on it and by clicking on a number you can listen to a representative speaker from the particular location. This option is similar in design to that for lexical sets (see previous paragraph).

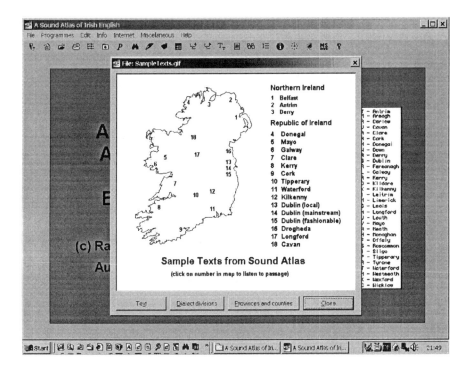

The fourth option is labelled *Sound file extracts*. The idea here is to offer a selection of sound file extracts which illustrate salient features of Irish English. The extracts are embedded in a text which displays information on the phonology of Irish English in a structured manner. This text is essentially that of section 6. *Extracts from sound files* above.

The fifth option in the *All choices* menu will display a tree with a selection of the sound files from the entire collection. This selection consists of some 270 samples divided into two levels. The idea of the selection is to offer users a first orientation in different forms of Irish English without confusing them with too much data. Here the branches of the tree correspond to the counties in Ireland. Below each county node there is a further branch called *More sound files*. This allows you access to a further selection of sound files from the county in question.

The next option will display all the sound files from the sound atlas. The organisation here is also geographical with nodes in the tree corresponding to provinces (4) and then to counties (32). There are over 1,500 sound files in the complete data set.

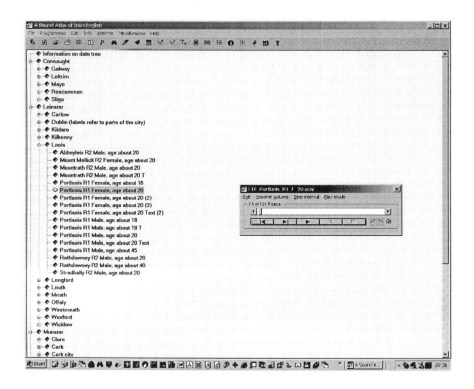

The final option loads a separate programme which provides an interface to *A Survey of Irish English Usage*. This survey covers the areas of morphology and syntax within Irish English and was conducted over a period of some years parallel to the collection of sound recordings. The survey was based on a questionnaire containing 57 sentences embodying structures typical of Irish English (see detailed description in section IV *A Survey of Irish English Usage* below).

There follows a description of the options available in the software interface to *A Sound Atlas of Irish English*. The description is organised on the basis of the menus to be found at the top of the screen.

1.2.2. Command description

General

List of all options [Ctrl-A] The easiest way to begin using *A Sound Atlas of Irish English* is to choose the present item which will show you all the options which are available within the programme. You can start with an introduction to Irish English and you can then listen to sample texts or a selection of sound files, proceeding to all sound files if you wish. There is also a set of sound file extracts and an active map with over 50 lexical sets for 18 locations throughout Ireland.

Show preface [F12] Here you are shown the text which forms a preface to *A Sound Atlas of Irish English*. It explains briefly the working of the programme, the data contained on the DVD and the options which are at your disposal from within *A Sound Atlas of Irish English*.

Load default data set [Ctrl-D] This option is a short cut to start the default data set for *A Sound Atlas of Irish English*. The factory setting for this is the data set with all sound files. However, you can determine this yourself if you like, setting it to the selection of sound files, for instance.

Open a data set [Ctrl-O] A list of the available data sets for *A Sound Atlas of Irish English* is displayed here allowing easy selection of a data set of your choice. This option is really only necessary if you have created you own data set(s). Otherwise use *List of all options*.

Information on set [Ctrl-I] A window with statistical information on the current data set is offered here.

Directory lister This option simply loads the directory lister without unloading the current data set. The purpose behind this option is primarily to allow you to check up on files on disk without the necessity of unloading the data set you are currently viewing.

Grid of recordings [F4] Assuming that you have loaded a group of sound files, then the current option will display all of these in the form of a grid. You can sort the grid by clicking on the heading for a particular column. By these means you can consult, say, all the word list or free text readings in the current data set.

County tiles [F5] This option shows you all 32 counties of Ireland as a set of tiles across the screen. Click on any county you wish to zoom in on. This will then show you a larger map of this county and a list of all recordings available in *A Sound Atlas of Irish English* for this part of the country is shown.

County statistics [Shift-F5] Here you are shown the locations where recordings were made for *A Sound Atlas of Irish English*. In brackets the number of sound files per location is indicated. As Dublin has a large surface area and encompasses about one third of the population of the Republic of Ireland, the regions of metropolitan Dublin are indicated as well.

Unload current data set [Ctrl-U] The currently loaded data set is removed with the present option. You notice this because the background image is visible again.

Reset default data set This option will reset the name of the default data set SoundAtlasIrishEnglish.dts (its original value). The programme also checks whether the default data set exists on disk.

Exit programme [Alt-F4] Unloads *A Sound Atlas of Irish English* after user confirmation.

Programmes

Survey of Irish English Usage [F8] This option will load a supplied programme which contains grammatical information from over 1,000 questionnaires which cover all the key morphological and syntactical structures of Irish English (see section IV *A Survey of Irish English Usage* below). The programme offers an interface to the data in the questionnaires which are present on the DVD in the form of databases. It allows users to view the returns for the questions, displaying these in chart form for visual effectiveness.

Directory for programmes / files [Shift-F8] Here you can specify the locations of two directories which are used by *A Sound Atlas of Irish English*. The present values are shown in the text boxes for the appropriate directories.

1)   Application files path
2)   Data files path

Of these two locations, the second is the more important. *A Sound Atlas of Irish English* expects all data files to be located below a folder node which by default will be C:\Program Files\A Sound Atlas of Irish English\SAIE_Data. If you have deposited the data from the DVD anywhere else then this will have to be conveyed to the programme via the current option.

Database editor By default this is *SAIE_Db,* the supplied database editor of the current programme suite. At this point you can choose another database editor which will then be used by *A Sound Atlas of Irish English.*

Make a database A supplied programme – *SAIE_MkDb* – enables you to create a database, or alter the structure of an existing one. The current option will load this programme and allow you to design a new database.

Generate a report form When exporting data from a database it is normally necessary to use a so-called report form which will determine the manner in which fields and their contents are transferred to an output text file. There is a supplied report form – DEFAULT.DBR – which illustrates how the process of exporting database contents works when availing of a report form. This file can also be edited with the report form editor – *SAIE_RepDb* – which is part of the current programme suite and which is loaded with the present option.

What file interface An extended file interface is included in the current programme and offers features not present in the standard interface offered by Windows. Specifically, the extended file interface shows you a tree of the current drive and so makes it easier to recognise where you are located in terms of branches and folders. By default the internal file interface is used. If you choose 'No' here the Windows interface will be used until possibly changed at a later date.

Your programme [F9] This option allows you to load a programme of your choice. When this terminates an automatic return to the outset is made.

Set your programme The programme you wish to run via F9 can be specified at this point. The name and full path of the programme are stored in the initialisation file so that you do not need to repeat this procedure for each work session.

Load jotter There is an internal text editor in *A Sound Atlas of Irish English* which can be loaded via the current command. As the name implies, it is intended for taking notes while working with the programme. The module can handle both plain text and Rich Text Format (RTF) files.

Load word processor [Ctrl-T] There is a supplied word processor with *A Sound Atlas of Irish English,* called *SAIE_WPro,* which can handle RTF, HTM and plain text files and which is loaded at this point. You can use *SAIE_WPro* to process almost any text files you wish except those which stem from a specific commercial word processor (first use the RTF format to store such files before attempting to load them with *SAIE_WPro*).

Specify your word processor You can change the default setting – *SAIE_WPro* – for your word processor with the present option. All you need do is locate the other programme on your hard disk. The name of the word processor is stored in the initialisation file and so maintained across work sessions.

Start file manager [Ctrl-M] This option will load the supplied file manager of the current package with which you can carry out various housekeeping tasks on the files of your computer, such as copying, moving, renaming, duplicating, or deleting.

Edit

Find string in tree nodes [Ctrl-F] Here you can search for any contents in the nodes of the currently loaded data set. When a string is found, the node is highlighted. It is sufficient to enter part of a node entry to find it.

Next occurrence of string [Ctrl-N] This option will repeat a search to continue looking for finds further down the data set tree, assuming that you have already entered a search string.

Expand tree This command will open up the leaves of the data tree by one level.

Collapse tree Similar to the previous option, but in the opposite direction, i.e. this command closes leaves in the data tree by one level.

Toggle screen font size There are two font sizes available for tree display, a standard font and a slightly larger one.

Info

Sample sentences The set of sentences which were presented to the informants who supplied readings are shown here. The file which is necessary for this option is: SAIE_Lex_Sets_Sentences.rtf.

Lexical sets A text showing the lexical sets – originally proposed by J. C. Wells in 1982 and modified somewhat for the current project – are displayed here. The file which is necessary for this option is: SAIE_Lex_Sets_Charts.rtf.

Word list Here a word list is shown which was used for some recordings of Dublin English, but not for the rest of the country (the latter recordings were made earlier). The idea was to have informants read aloud a set of words in careful style which contain key sounds of Irish English. The file which is necessary for this option is: SAIE_WordList.rtf.

Free text This is a stretch of free text which was devised especially for this project and which contains the sounds of Irish English including many which are crucial to present-day changes in Irish English. The file which is necessary for this option is: SAIE_FreeText.rtf.

Overview of Irish English This option offers an overview of the history and present-day forms of Irish English. The file which is necessary for this option is: Overview_IE.htm.

Issues in Irish English studies A list of those linguistic issues which have been central to Irish English studies and which have been discussed in recent literature is offered here. The file which is necessary for this option is: Issues_IE.htm.

References for Irish English Here a set of bibliographical references for Irish English studies is offered. The file which is necessary for this option is: REFERENCES.HTM.

References for phonology This option presents a set of references referring specifically to the study of Irish English phonology. The file which is necessary for this option is: SAIE_Bib_Phonology.rtf.

Landmarks in Irish history A text file with information on the history of Ireland is displayed here; the required file is called HISTORY.RTF and is expected to reside in the same directory as the main programme.

History of Irish English Information on the history of Irish English is shown here; the required file is called IR_ENG_H.RTF and is expected to reside in the same directory as the main programme.

Biographical notes Some information on important figures in Irish English studies is displayed here. The required file is called BIOGRAPH.RTF and is expected to reside in the same directory as the main programme.

Journals of interest A selection of journals which are of relevance to the study of Irish English can be viewed here; the required file is called JOURNALS.RTF and is expected to reside in the same directory as the main programme.

Glossary for Irish English A list of terms which are germane to the study of Irish English is offered here. The required file is called

GLOSSARY.RTF and is expected to reside in the same directory as the main programme.

Internet

Browse on web This option will activate an internal web browser with which you can navigate through the internet without exiting *A Sound Atlas of Irish English*. There is a history function and you can maintain a list of the web site addresses you might want to visit.

Send an email Here the programme which is designated as the default email application on your system is loaded and you can work with this as you wish. When you terminate this application an automatic return to the current programme is made.

Miscellaneous

Get background image If you do not want to use the default image supplied with the current programme you can choose another image file (with the extension .JPG, .BMP or .GIF) at this point.

Form background colour The colour used for the background of the main desktop area can be determined here.

Date and time Simply displays the current date and time in the centre of the screen.

Pocket calculator Activates the internal calculator in *A Sound Atlas of Irish English*.

Find a file This option opens a dialogue in which you can enter the name of a file you are looking for. Alternatively you can type a file template, such as *.RTF, and the programme will return any finds on your disk, displaying them in the file box at the bottom of the window.

Browse among multimedia files With the current option the directory lister is activated and you can view image files or hear audio files which may be present on your disk.

Adjust volume of speaker Activates the volume control of Windows to allow you to set the volume to the level suitable for your audio system.

Sound player to use Under Microsoft Windows you can listen to sound tracks which are deposited in special files, usually with the extension WAV. Such files can be processed directly by the sound recorder which is part of the standard group of Windows programmes. However, the sound files either created with the sound recorder or which can be processed by it are unnecessarily large as are the graphic files in the standard Windows bitmap format. For this reason other researchers have developed compression techniques to greatly reduce the size without any noticeable loss in quality. With graphic files, the compressed format used in JPG files has become generally accepted and is widely used on the Internet. With sound files, there is a similar compression standard. This was developed by the *Frauenhofer Gesellschaft*, a research institute in Germany, and the technique used is known as MPEG Layer 3 or simply 'MP3'. This can reduce a sound file to over one tenth of its original size without altering the quality noticeably. In order to playback sound files on your computer which have been encoded using this technique you require a software filter known as an MPEG Layer 3 Audio Decoder. There is one available directly from the Frauenhofer Gesellschaft through a software firm they co-operate with. But recently Microsoft has been offering to its customers a special Windows *Media Player* with an MPEG Layer 3 filter included. As of versions 6.4 and higher of this programme, compressed audio files can be played back without difficulty. If you wish, you can download the latest version of the Windows *Media Player* from the Internet (there is an option in the 'Go' menu of the player to jump straight to the appropriate home page).

You can specify which sound player you wish to use in the current programme by selecting either the Windows *Media Player* or the inbuilt audio playback module (in which case you leave the input line empty). The latter is slightly faster and will work if you already have an MPEG Layer 3 Audio Decoder installed on your computer (this is automatically available in more recent versions of Windows). The way to find out this is quite simple: see if the sound files work without choosing an external programme. If they do not, choose the Windows *Media Player* to ensure they do.

Set colour for tree The colour used when viewing a data tree can be determined with the current option.

Database colour Via the current option the background colour for the cells of a database can be set.

Colour for text display Lastly, the colour used when any text is displayed in a separate window can be decided upon with this option. All these colour values are stored in the initialisation file.

About this programme This displays a small text about *A Sound Atlas of Irish English* and identifies the author and publisher.

Help

Open explorer window [Shift-Ctrl-F9] This option will open an explorer window and logs in the current directory. You can use this for any file manipulation (copying, moving, deleting) you might wish to do. Be careful, however, if you manipulate files or folders which are presently in use as this can disturb the operation of the current programme.

    Main help text Here you can load the help file.

    Show start tips There is a small supplied text file which can be displayed when the current programme is first loaded. It gives the user some useful hints about what to do. Once you have read it once or twice you will probably not need it any more and may choose not to have it displayed on startup. With the current option you can nonetheless view this file without altering the situation on loading.

    Troubleshooting tips This option will load a text file, SAIE_TRSH.RTF, which contains advice on difficulties which users might experience when working with *A Sound Atlas of Irish English*. In case you cannot start *A Sound Atlas of Irish English* at all, you should consult this file using your own word processor (the text is also contained in this book, see section V *Technical notes* below). It is a normal text file in Rich Text Format and can be read by nearly all commercially available word processors such as Microsoft *Word* or *WordPerfect*.

    Remove A Sound Atlas of Irish English A small text is displayed here which describes the three steps which are necessary to remove all the files of the current programme suite from your computer.

    Make desktop folder You can create a folder for your Windows desktop with the current option. It calls a small programme which will make the folder and insert links to the various programmes of the current suite. The important point about this utility is that it takes into account the language-specific location of the *A Sound Atlas of Irish English* software, i.e. it uses the particular value for the *Program Files* directory which is used on your computer, e.g. Program Files in English, but Programme in German, etc.

    Computer terms A glossary of common computer terms which the user might wish to check up on is displayed with the present option. The list is contained in a text file called COMPDICT.RTF which is expected to be located in the home directory of the current programme.

2. Further programmes

The Windows programme suite supplied with *A Sound Atlas of Irish English* contains a number of additional utilities which can be used for various tasks which may arise when using the sound atlas. In the following a brief description of each is offered. For every programme there is a comprehensive help file which can always be accessed by pressing F1. The commands are in general those which one would expect from a Windows application.

2.1. File Manager

The idea behind this programme is to allow users to view data files directly from the directory on disk where they are located and possibly copy, move or delete these as well. The programme is reminiscent in its structure of the Windows *Explorer* in that it uses a hierarchical tree in which all information about drives and directories is stored. There is also a special file copying level which offers additional functionality useful for file management purposes.

The programme has a range of options which makes it flexible enough to cater for the needs of many users when viewing files. Most of these are intuitively obvious in the manner in which they function – the simplest is the SpaceBar command which will display virtually any file. Bear in mind that the most common commands can be executed by clicking on the symbol in the toolbar immediately below the menu bar at the top of the screen, others can be accessed via the right mouse button.

2.2. Word Processor

The current programme is a flexible word processor which allows you to edit any number of texts in a variety of formats. The main one is RTF – *rich text format* – a text encoding protocol used widely on personal computers and supported by nearly all vendors of commercial software. The word processor also permits the processing of texts written in HTML – *Hypertext Markup Language*, that used for Internet applications – as well as ASCII texts (unformatted) and its own native format.

You can convert between these types with ease. In addition, data from Microsoft *Word* can be pasted directly into any text you are processing. Apart from the many formatting options, the word processor also has an inbuilt database interface, an outline text browser, calendar, etc.

2.3. Database Editor

The present programme offers a quick and efficient way to process databases. The programme contains the options necessary for basic editing of databases. There are a few additional features which make it an alternative to other database editors. For instance, the macro facility which allows the insertion of pre-defined pieces of text into the current cell (the row and column corresponding to the current field of the present record of the database you are editing). Another feature is the text editor component which operates parallel to the database engine. For any database you load the programme will load a text of the same name (but with the extension .RTF) and then maintains this in tandem with the database. You can thus use the accompanying text as a repository for data which you do not wish to enter into a field of the database (perhaps because of its peripheral and/or unstructured nature). This text can be printed and stored on disk under a user-specified name.

Note that any changes made to the contents of a database are automatically saved to disk. This is normal procedure with databases as the contents of all records are not maintained in memory – unlike text editors which copy the entire contents of a file to memory before you process this. The databases which you process with the database editor must be in the *dBASE* format, a type which is understood by the majority of commercial database managers. You can export any selection of records to an output text which can be stored in Rich Text Format which means that it can be read by virtually any commercial text editor or word processor. Such files can also be transferred via the internet without any difficulty, e.g. as an attachment to an email. Exporting can be done using a report form which will arrange the data contained in the records of the database in a user-specified manner (see programme *Report Database* for details of how to construct and use a report form).

2.4. Make Database

With this programme users can design new databases easily and efficiently. The programme will generate databases in the *dBASE* format which is the native format of the supplied database editor of *A Sound Atlas of Irish English* (see previous section). When the programme starts you are presented with a screen on which there are four list boxes. Each of these corresponds to the four items of information which are required for the structure of a database. If you wish, you can select a database to act as a model for the one you are currently constructing. When you have finished entering / altering the information for all the fields of the database you can generate this and save the structure to disk.

2.5. Report Form Generator

This programme is a utility with which users can determine just how the data from fields of a database is arranged when exported to a text file. The programme is intended to work with databases in the *dBASE* format which is the native format of the database module of *A Sound Atlas of Irish English* (see above). Recall to begin with that a database is a set of records each consisting of a set number of fields.

Database	*Record*
Set of records	Number of fields filled with specific data

When exporting the contents of the records to a text file you can specify (1) what fields are exported, e.g. only a selection if you wish, and (2) whether extraneous text is also inserted in the text file which is generated. This export procedure can be conceived of as an operation during which the contents of a database are sent through a report form before reaching the destination of a text file or the Windows clipboard. The report form is thus a kind of filter determining what the output actually looks like.

Input		*Filter*		*Output*
Database	→	Report Form	→	Text file

Report form generators vary greatly in the options they offer. The current programme allows users to specify such information as the font attributes to be used for a field and the extraneous text to be included to the left and right of any field. Within the programme you have access to a comprehensive help file which contains much information about how to avail of report forms.

IV *A Survey of Irish English Usage*

1. Introduction

This survey covers the areas of morphology and syntax within Irish English and was conducted over a period of several years parallel to the collection of sound recordings. The survey was based on a questionnaire of some 57 sample sentences, each of which contains a structure which is known to occur in some form of Irish English. Informants were asked to judge the sentences in terms of acceptance in casual speech among friends. They were told that the survey was about colloquial speech, not written English. The questionnaire was only done in groups of two or more as informants tended to be much less prescriptive in groups than as individuals. There were basically three types of answer which allowed for grading of acceptability. Informants could specify that a given sentence represented *no problem*, was *a bit strange* or indeed was *unacceptable*. The vast majority of informants were in the 18-30 age bracket. This was deliberate as the goal of the survey was to determine the acceptance of certain structures in colloquial speech among the younger generation of Irish.

Approximately 80% of returned questionnaires were actually used. There are over 1,000 questionnaires, collected over a period of several years, which were acceptable (1,017 in all). The criterion for acceptance was the following: each questionnaire must have all three categories used, e.g. any informant who ticked 'no problem' for all sentences was ignored as well as anyone who said that all sentences were 'a bit strange' or 'unacceptable' as this showed a lack of discrimination on the part of the individual in question. The spread among categories must have been at least 10%. Naturally, all sentences must have been evaluated and the questionnaires of those informants who inserted prescriptive comments were ignored. The headings of the questionnaire, indicating its structure (see below), were not included in the version given to informants.

It is known from sociolinguistic surveys, that informants show a degree of fatigue towards the end of an interview or when filling out a questionnaire. For this reason, structures which were not too important were put on the last page of the questionnaire, e.g. focus markers and minor points of usage which contrast with English, such as the use of *shall* for the future or *do* support with *use*. In quite a number of instances, the author noticed that informants ticked off the last sentences very quickly and frequently with the same value. Anyone who did this, for instance, who said that he/she had no problem with *Did you used to cycle to school?* were asked if this was really the case. In quite a number of instances, informants revised their judgements, though not always in the Dublin area and in Northern Ireland.

2. Processing software

The purpose of the present programme is to offer users of *A Survey of Irish English Usage* an easy-to-use interface with which they can examine the data which has been entered into the databases which form the basis for the survey. Each of these databases contains the data of one questionnaire and there are 1,017 databases in all, corresponding to the number of questionnaires which were evaluated.

The programme has two main levels. The first is one where the questionnaire databases can be analysed. You do this by choosing sample sentences and then consider their distribution across one or more counties. The results are displayed in a separate window and you can copy the output text to the Windows clipboard and from there to your word processor, for example. The results can be viewed as a bar chart and this can also be copied to the Windows clipboard or stored to disk so that any chart with any set of results can equally be inserted into a text you might be preparing in which you would like to integrate data from an interrogation of *A Survey of Irish English Usage*.

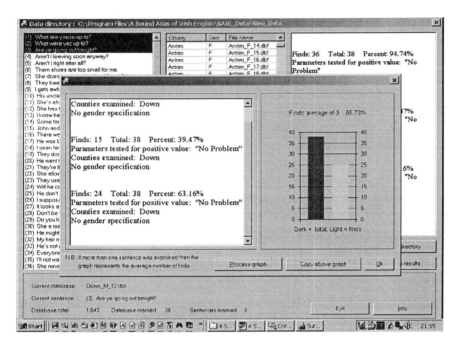

The second level of the programme will display the questionnaire databases in a special window and you can navigate at will in the set. This option has been offered because users might want to see how the informants evaluated the sentences they were presented with. All 1,017 questionnaire databases are contained on the DVD and can be viewed directly.

File

Analyse databases [Ctrl-A] This option allows you to interrogate the databases of the survey to see what the acceptance of any sentence or sentences is like in any county or counties. Sentences and counties are selected in the lists provided in the centre of the screen in the usual manner: you mark items in a list by holding the Ctrl-key depressed and clicking the left mouse button. You can also select databases by province via the option *Select databases.* When you then click on the button *Analyse databases* you can choose the parameters for which the databases are to be examined. These are (1) *No problem,* (2) *A bit strange* and (3) *Unacceptable*. Parameters can be combined, for instance you could check for positive values with the first two parameters if you wish. Furthermore, you can specify whether you wish questionnaires from informants of both genders to be considered or only female or only male. Counties can be analysed individually (if specified) otherwise the average returns for the counties you selected will be displayed.

When the returns are displayed in the results window you will notice that there is a text section on the left with information on the search (you can mark any piece of text and copy it to the Windows clipboard in the usual manner, click the right mouse button for the necessary commands). There is also a graph on the right. This graph contains combined results, for instance, if you interrogate the databases using more than one sentence, then the average returns are displayed here.

In the results window you will notice a button labelled *Process graph*. Click here to have a detailed chart displayed. The first thing which happens is a window with the parameters for the chart is shown. Normally you will not have to change anything here, just click on the button *Make chart*. But you can experiment with different options, for instance, colours, background, size, etc. for the graph to be generated. Any changes can be stored to disk and loaded at a future date. Click on the *Help* button in this window for further information.

Browse databases [Ctrl-B] On choosing this option a large window opens in which a tree of the current drive and a file listing is displayed. Assuming that the current folder is where the questionnaire databases are located then the contents of the databases are displayed on the right. Move the bar up and down in the middle window (the file listing) to view the contents of different databases. If nothing is displayed in the middle or right window, select the drive and folder where the databases are located by clicking on a drive and/or folder.

Information on databases [Ctrl-I] This option will show you the databases for the various provinces and counties along with the distribution across genders. The information in the grid can be stored to the Windows clipboard. When you copy this to your word processor you may need to set the width of tabulators for the columns to be aligned correctly.

Directory lister The purpose behind this option is primarily to allow you to check up on files on disk without the necessity of exiting the programme.

Exit programme [Alt-F4] Unloads *A Survey of Irish English Usage* after user confirmation.

Interface

Open explorer window [Shift-Ctrl-F9] This option will open an explorer window and logs in the current directory. You can use this for any file manipulation (copying, moving, deleting) you might wish to do.

Your programme [F9] This option allows you to load a programme of your choice. When this terminates an automatic return to the outset is made.

Set your programme The programme you wish to run via F9 can be specified at this point. The name and full path of the programme are stored in the initialisation file so that you do not need to repeat this procedure for each work session.

Folder for auxiliary files This command allows you to specify the directory in which various files, used internally by the current programme, are located. This location is noted and maintained across work sessions.

Date and time Simply displays the current date and time in the centre of the screen.

Information

Background to A Survey of Irish English Usage Here a text is shown which explains the approach used when collecting and evaluating data for the current survey.

Questionnaire text The set of 57 sentences which the informants were presented with for the survey are shown here. The text displayed here contains labels indicating what grammatical features were contained in the sentences, divided according to linguistic levels. Needless to say, the informants were not presented with this information as they were not supposed to know what structures might be contained in which sentences.

Counties of Ireland A map of north and south Ireland showing the names of the 32 counties is displayed here.

References for Irish English A selection of bibliographical references for the study of Irish English is offered here. For more information, please consult the items mentioned at the beginning of this text.

Help

Help text Here you can load the help text file.

About this programme Displays a small text about *A Survey of Irish English Usage* and identifies the author.

Generating and processing charts

In the chart settings window you are shown quite an amount of information which is used to generate the chart with the results of your search. Normally you will not have to change anything here, as the information is inserted automatically by the programme, just click on the button *Make chart*. But you can experiment with different options, for instance, colours, background, size, etc. for the graph to be generated. Any changes can be stored to disk and loaded at a future date. The following is a brief description of what the different options do and how / if they should be filled or altered.

Row values This entry should be left empty unless you wish to generate sets of columns for your chart or several pies for a pie chart. The programme does not do this automatically, choosing instead to display each set of results separately.

Column values Here the results of each run with a search are entered automatically as a list of numbers, either percentages or relative totals, representing the acceptance of the sentences marked before the analysis was carried out. Do not change these values.

Labels for bar charts The text snippets found here are automatically entered and are linked to the column values in the line above. They either represent the sentences which were selected for an analysis or the names of counties, if you select one sentence and demand an analysis by individual county. You may change these values, but do *not* alter the number of labels, each separated by a semi-colon. If you want to, try this and see the results by generating a chart

Text for X-axis The text here will be displayed horizontally below the chart. Either a reference to the gender specification is displayed or the sentence, if a single sentence and analysis by individual county is chosen.

Text for title of chart The title is shown at the top of the chart and can be specified here.

Fonts for chart labels Different labels around the resulting chart can appear in user-specified fonts. Try changing values here to see what happens.

Chart size If you select several sentences, or many counties (for analysis by individual counties and not county average) then you may find that the size you have chosen is not large enough. The maximum you can choose depends on the resolution of the screen. Choose *Max* and see if this is enough, otherwise, try changing the resolution via the *Display* parameters by clicking *Settings* in the *Start* menu on the Windows desktop.

Chart type By default a bar chart is chosen for display. You can also have a pie chart shown which, depending on the purpose of the chart, might be a sensible alternative.

Use colours You may choose to display the columns in black or in different colours. If you are importing the results into a word processor, then black columns might well be best.

Use white background The background can be either white or grey. If you are choosing not to use colours, i.e. to have black columns, then a white background is preferable.

Settings file All the values which can be specified in this window can be stored to disk under a file name of your choice and with the automatic extension .chs (= *chart settings*). The reverse is also possible, i.e. you can load values from a file previously stored to disk.

3. The survey and Irish English

The grammar of Irish English has been the object of considerable attention in the past 20 years or so. The scholars who have investigated the subject matter can be broadly divided into two camps. On the one hand there are those who see in the language shift from Irish to English as the main source of all idiosyncratic structures in this variety of English (see Bliss 1972, 1977, 1984). On the other hand there are scholars who look to the archaic and regional inputs of English to Ireland to discern sources for specific features of Irish English (see Harris 1983, 1984, 1993; Lass 1990). These two approaches have been dubbed the *substratist* and *retentionist* standpoints respectively (Filppula 1993). If one considers the grammatical structures of Irish English then there are very few for which one can claim only an Irish source. This has been emphasised repeatedly by scholars of the retentionist persuasion. But for all other grammatical idiosyncrasies one can in fact point to both sources so that in many cases we may be dealing with instances of convergence (Hickey 1995, 1997).

There is one further approach which in the past few years has gained favour among linguists. This is the typological standpoint which stresses structural similarities between Irish and English and which sees the island of Ireland, if not in fact the entire British Isles, as a linguistic area (Wagner 1959). In this respect one could quote Hickey (1999a) and Vennemann (2000, 2001). There are indeed many parallels between the two languages. For instance, in Irish and English in the north of the country one has a very front realisation of the GOOSE vowel. In both Irish and conservative varieties of Irish English one has a distinction of short vowels before /r/. On a more abstract level one may find that the parallels are a matter of principle but not of exponence (Hickey 1997). For instance, Irish has an extensive system of lenition and Irish English shows clear lenition of alveolars in relatively open positions (Hickey 1996). Certainly the manifestation of these two phenomena is quite different in each language but one could say that there is a similar phonological directive to lenite elements in positions of high sonority in both cases.

On the levels of morphology and syntax the parallels between Irish and English are even more obvious so that one can justifiably posit convergence as a factor in language change in Ireland. For example, one finds in both cases a distinction between the second person singular and plural pronouns. In syntax there are many similarities, for instance in the system of aspectual distinctions which hold in each language. Both Irish and English have a perfective and an habitual aspect. It is true that these are realised quite differently in each case, but the categories are similar in scope in each language. Another syntactic feature one could point out here is the existence of a continuous verb form in both Irish and English. A further feature would be the range of the present tense, the use of 'for to' with the infinitive or the common occurrence of negative concord (multiple negation). For a more detailed presentation of possible sources, see various discussions below.

In order to help scholars to arrive at a considered view of what could be a possible contact phenomenon and what a dialect retention, the present survey can be used. To this end the informants are classified by county so one can choose to examine the relative acceptance of struc-tures suspected of being contact phenomena from Irish in those counties in which Irish is still spoken or where it was found to some degree during of the 20th century. Furthermore, one could look at the acceptance of structures in counties of Northern Ireland which are known to have had significant degrees of Ulster Scots settlement.

Of course apart from the consideration of contact versus dialect as a source for specific features, the survey can be used generally to see what the acceptance of putatively Irish English features is like with members of the younger generation in present-day Ireland.

3.1. Analysis of questionnaire

The following paragraphs discuss the features which were embedded into the sentences of the questionnaire used for the survey. The questionnaire as it was offered to the test persons is given in the next section but one.

Morphology

Second person plural This is a feature which occurs in both Irish and Irish English. In the latter there are basically three options: (1) *ye*, the old original input form of early modern English (also found in north-east England, see Beal 1993), (2) *youse*, a constructed plural probably originating with speakers of Irish during the language shift period and (3) *yez*, which is a combination of both. The Irish second person plural pronoun is *sibh*. See Hickey (2003d) for a detailed discussion of second person plural pronouns in many varieties of English.

Negation of auxiliaries The contraction of *am* and *not* normally yields *amn't* in Irish English, other forms like *ain't* and *aren't* are unusual.

Demonstrative pronouns The use of the demonstrative pronoun *them* as a plural marker has a long history in English. This usage was probably carried to Ireland and continues to this day. There is no question of influence from Irish in this respect.

Syntax

1) Aspectual distinctions

Habitual aspect There are basically two ways of indicating habitual aspect in Irish English. The first is to use an unstressed form of *do* with *be*. The second is to use an inflected form of *be*. The latter method is found particularly in Northern Ireland whereas the former is far more common in the south. When considering the question of dialect or retention, one must bear in mind that the formal manifestation of the habitual in Irish is quite different from that in Irish English. Nonetheless one could perhaps postulate that native speakers of Irish transferred the category of habitual to the English they were learning in the language shift period, approximately between the beginning of the 17th to the late 19th centuries. There is, however, one serious difficulty with this assumption, that is that the historical records show no documentation for the habitual – in either form – before the middle of the 19th century (Hickey 2005). The alternative explanation is that the habitual was taken to Ireland with input from the South-West and in general, West Midlands of England. Whether one is dealing with a full-blown aspectual distinction from an English source or simply with unstressed positive *do* which was then 'usurped' by the Irish for this purpose (Hickey 1995, 1997) is very difficult to decide.

Immediate perfective There are two types of perfective aspect in Irish English. The first of these refers to an action which has just happened and which has highly informational value. This is the so-called immediate perfective. There is no doubt that this is a transfer structure from Irish where the temporal adverb *tar éis* 'after' is found with a following non-finite verb clause to indicate that something has just happened.

Resultative perfective The second type of perfective is used to indicate that a generally known goal has been reached. It avails of a word order in which the non-finite verb form is placed after the object. This then contrasts with the normal word order of English in which the verb precedes the object. Hence the sentence *Have you the novel read?* implies that both the hearer and the speaker are aware of the intention of the latter to read a novel and the inquiry is whether this action has been completed, that is whether the result has been reached. The word order with the non-finite verb form after the object is the only word order in Irish but it may also have been present in input forms of English in the early modern period.

2) Tense range and forms

Extended present In both Irish and Irish English the present tense has a wider range than in more standard forms of English. Specifically, it is used to encompass the time range expressed by the present perfect in English. For example *I know him for several years now* would illustrate this extended use of the present tense.

Present-tense marking As might be expected the subject concord rule in forms of Irish English is different from standard English. The situation is slightly different in the north and the south of the country. But the generalisation seems to be valid for Irish English as a whole that plural subjects are given singular inflection, e.g. *The girls gets tired of that rough talk.*

Singular existential Related to the previous phenomenon is the use of a singular verb in existential sentences despite a plural reference, e.g. *There was plenty of people interested in buying the house.*

Epistemic negative The negative of *must* in an epistemic sense is *can't* in standard English. In the Irish English, however, the form *mustn't* is found. This probably resulted from an extension from the positive to the negative by speakers during the language shift.

Past tense verb forms In common with many non-standard varieties of English, Irish English also shows a reduced number of forms in the past. The two most common instances of this are *seen* and *done* which are used as simple past forms.

'For to' infinitives In particular with verbs of purpose, infinitives are formed with 'for to' in Irish English as in *He went to Dublin for to buy a car.* Irish uses a similar word *chun* 'in order to' at the head of a non-finite verb clause in equivalent sentences.

'Be' auxiliary The use of *be* as an auxiliary is clearly an archaic feature of Irish English, for example *We are finished our dinner* for *We have finished our dinner.*

Infinitive without 'to' One of the major differences in grammar between the north and the south of Ireland is the occurrence of certain infinitival complements without *to* in southern Irish English, as in *He was allowed go home.*

Uninflected auxiliaries A feature of conservative east coast dialects is that the verbs *do* and *have* are not inflected when they function as auxiliaries, e.g. *He have all the work done.* This does not apply when one is dealing with these verbs in a lexical function.

Conditional modals The point being tested with this particular sentence was whether *might* can occur as a conditional in Irish English.

Imperatives with continuous form A well attested feature of Irish English, which in fact goes back further than the first attestations of the habitual aspect, is the use of a continuous verb form in imperatives such as *Don't be worrying about the children.*

Interrogative 'do'-support The use of *do* with interrogatives in English is optional and this question was intended to determine the reaction of informants to interrogative sentences with *do* support.

Copula deletion A feature which has occasionally been attested in Irish English from the south-east of the country is the deletion of a copula in equative sentences. The reaction of informants to such sentences was tested here.

Double modals A feature which has only been recorded for the north of Ireland and which is decidedly recessive even there is the use of two modals in a single clause or sentence as *He might could come after all.* This feature was apparently transported to the New World and continues to exist in forms of English in the south-east of the United States (Montgomery 2001).

Verb complements A significant feature of English in Northern Ireland is the use of a past participle as a complement to the verb *need*, e.g. *My hair needs washed.* In the south of Ireland a continuous form of the verb is used here instead.

3) Negation

Negative concord Most vernacular forms of Irish English allow for negative concord, that is any element within a clause which can occur in the negative will do so if the entire clause is negative, e.g. *He isn't interested in no cars.* In the supraregional form of Irish English multiple negation does not occur.

Lack of negative attraction In both the north and the south of Ireland a lack of negative attraction is typical of vernacular varieties, as in *Everyone didn't want to leave* for *Nobody wanted to leave.*

Negator contraction A lack of negator contraction is something which is associated with Scottish English nowadays. However, this appears also to have been characteristic of Irish English previously. For example,

Sean O'Casey in his plays uses this feature quite frequently, e.g. *She'll not come this evening*. In supraregional varieties of Irish English this type of structure does not occur.

Singular reference 'never' A feature of all forms of Irish English is the use of the word *never* with singular time reference, for example *He never rang me yesterday evening*. The source of this feature is not absolutely certain but it should be said that punctual reference is also found in Irish with the word *riamh* 'never'. The occurrence in Scottish English could also be traced to Gaelic influence perhaps, although this feature is also attested in various dialects of English English.

4) Clause structure

Relative clause marking The most common means of introducing a relative clause in Irish English is to use the word *that* (Corrigan 1997), irrespective of whether the referent is animate are not, e.g. *The man that was here yesterday said he will come back*. Within the context of Irish English there are two further possibilities here. The first is a zero relative and the second is the use of *what* with an animate referent.

Front clefting A significant parallel between Irish and Irish English is the use of clefts to topicalise some part of a sentence. An example would be *Is it to Galway you're going?* The scope of topicalisation via clefting is deemed to be greater in Irish English than in other varieties (Filppula 1999: Chapter 10).

Subordinating 'and' This feature quite definitely represents a transfer phenomenon from Irish as there is no structural model for it in the history of English, a very few attestations of something similar notwithstanding. The type of Irish sentence which provided the model here is seen in *Chuaigh sí amach agus é ag cur báistí.* lit. Went she out and it at putting rain-GENITIVE 'She went out and it raining'.

Embedded inversion The use of inversion in embedded interrogative sentences is quite typical of various forms of Irish English, that is the use of *if* before such embedded sentences can be avoided, e.g. *They asked her was she travelling abroad*.

Relevance via 'on' + pronoun This is a phenomenon which probably has a double source. On the one hand there are ample attestations from the history of English and from various overseas varieties, such as American or Australian English, both of which show a liberal use of the pronoun *on* to express relevance of an action. But the same is true of Irish which uses a similar construction repeatedly, as seen in a sentence like *Thit an dréimire orm* 'The ladder fell down on me' which can have both a literal and a figurative interpretation, the latter being 'The ladder I was attending fell down'.

5) Determiners, numerals

Over-use of definite article The occurrence of the definite article with nouns which are used in a generic sense is a typical feature of Irish English, e.g. *He likes the life in Dublin.* The definite article is also found with languages, institutions, and various kinds of subject matter. For a full treatment of this feature, see Filppula (1999: Chapter 5).

Singular after numerals This is a widespread feature of many dialects of English, indeed for many languages it is the norm rather than the exception. It also occurs in Irish English but its diagnostic significance is very slight.

Unbound reflexives The present feature is obviously a transfer phenomenon from Irish where a reflexive pronoun can be used in sentence-initial position to refer to an individual who is regarded somehow as being the person in charge or the person in a leading position as in *An bhfuil sé féin isteach inniu?* lit. INTERROGATIVE is-RELATIVE he himself in today 'Is himself in today', i.e. the boss, the head of the house, etc. For a full treatment of this feature, see Filppula (1999: Chapter 5).

6) Adverbs, focus markers

Adverb marking There are a large range of intensifying adverbs used in Irish English, notably without the *-ly* inflection which is found in standard English. Here acceptance among informants was tested.

'Till' for 'until' The use of *till* in the sense of 'in order to' is a common feature of Irish English which has been remarked on frequently. It can be seen in a sentence like *Sit down till I tell you what I did.*

Sentence-final focus markers A number of markers are used, particularly in northern Irish English, to achieve focus at the end of a sentence. Here the acceptance of *but* in this function was tested.

7) Contrasting English usage

'Do' support with 'use' The verb *use* does not take the auxiliary *do* when forming the past tense or an interrogative sentence in Irish English. The acceptance of a sentence with *do* support was tested here.

'Shall' versus 'will' as future auxiliary When forming the future the auxiliary *will* is much preferred to *shall* in Irish English. Of course this only applies to cases where a non-contracted form is used.

3.2. Possible sources for features of Irish English

Given the debate concerning the importance of contact versus retention in the history of Irish English (Filppula 1993, Hickey 1995, 1997) it would seem appropriate at this point to offer suggestions concerning the sources of certain features which are regarded by scholars in the field as central to the grammatical profile of Irish English. It should be stressed here that the tables below derive from the opinions of the author and other scholars may well have different views on the possible sources of the features listed.

Morphological features

Distinct pronominal forms for second person singular and plural	Convergence of English input and Irish
Epistemic negative *must*	Generalisation made by the Irish based on positive use
Them as demonstrative	English input only

Syntactic features

Habitual aspect	Convergence with south-west English input on east coast, possibly with influence from Scots via Ulster. Otherwise transfer of category from Irish

Immediate perfective aspect with *after*	Transfer from Irish
Resultative perfective with OV word order	Possible convergence, primarily from Irish
Subordinating *and*	Transfer from Irish
Variant use of suffixal -*s* in present	South-west input in first period on east coast
Clefting for topicalisation	Transfer from Irish, with some possible convergence
Greater range of the present tense	Transfer from Irish, with some possible convergence
Negative concord	Convergence of English input and Irish
For to infinitives indicating purpose	Convergence of English input and Irish
Reduced number of verb forms	English input only
Be as auxiliary	English input only
Single time reference for *never*	Transfer from Irish, English input

3.3. Questionnaire for *A Survey of Irish English Usage*

Informants and classification

Test person   ☐ male   ☐ female
               ☐ under 18   ☐ 18 – 30   ☐ over 30   ☐ over 40
Home county:

How do you find the following sentences (in casual speech among your friends)?

no problem   a bit strange   unacceptable   something else, short comment:

☐   ☐   ☐

(Informants could tick one of the above boxes depending on how they felt about the structure in question. In a very few cases, informants added a short comment. In the questionnaire the boxes were to be found after each sentence below.)

Test sentences used for the survey

(1)   *What are youse up to?*
(2)   *What were yez up to?*
(3)   *Are ye going out tonight?*
(4)   *Amn't I leaving soon anyway?*
(5)   *Aren't I right after all?*
(6)   *Them shoes are too small for me.*
(7)   *She does be worrying about the children.*
(8)   *They bees up late at night.*
(9)   *I gets awful anxious about the kids at night.*
(10)   *His uncle does be a hard worker.*
(11)   *She's after spilling the milk.*
(12)   *She has the housework done.*
(13)   *I know her for five years now.*
(14)   *Some farmers has little or no cattle.*
(15)   *John and his wife plays bingo at the weekend.*
(16)   *There was two men on the road.*
(17)   *He was born here so he mustn't be Scottish.*
(18)   *I seen him yesterday.*
(19)   *They done all the work for us.*
(20)   *He went to Dublin for to buy a car.*
(21)   *They're finished the work now.*
(22)   *She allowed him drive the car.*
(23)   *They used make me stay in my room for hours.*
(24)   *Will he come see us in the spring?*
(25)   *He don't like me staying up late.*
(26)   *I suppose he have his work done now.*
(27)   *It looks as if it might rain, doesn't it?*
(28)   *Don't be teasing your brother.*
(29)   *Do you have any matches on you?*
(30)   *She a teacher in the new college.*
(31)   *He might could come after all.*
(32)   *My hair needs washed.*
(33)   *He's not interested in no cars.*
(34)   *Everyone didn't want to hear them.*
(35)   *I'll not wait any longer for him.*

(36)   *She never rang yesterday evening.*
(37)   *I know a farmer that rears sheep.*
(38)   *I know a farmer rears sheep.*
(39)   *I know a farmer what rears sheep.*
(40)   *It's to Glasgow he's going tomorrow.*
(41)   *We went for a walk and it raining.*
(42)   *She asked him was he interested.*
(43)   *He asked who had she spoken to.*
(44)   *He likes the life in Galway.*
(45)   *The fire went out on him.*
(46)   *He crashed the car on her.*
(47)   *She has to go to the hospital for a check-up.*
(48)   *Their youngest son is good at the maths.*
(49)   *I suppose the both of us should go.*
(50)   *He paid twenty pound for the meal.*
(51)   *Himself is not in today.*
(52)   *The work is real difficult.*
(53)   *Come here till I tell you.*
(54)   *She's hard-working, like.*
(55)   *He's gone to the races, but?*
(56)   *Did you use to cycle to school?*
(57)   *I shall have to leave soon.*

4. Java version of survey software

Users who have not installed the Windows software on their computer, or those who have an Apple *Macintosh* or are using the Linux operating system, may wish to examine the data of *A Survey of Irish English Usage*.

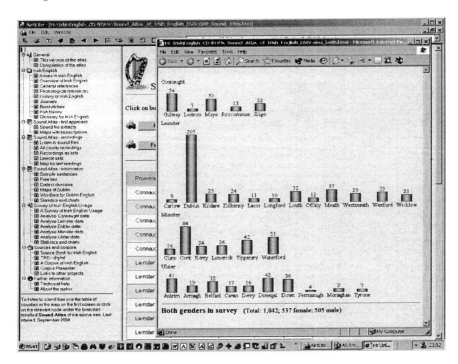

This is possible within the Java version of the software. The third branch from the bottom of the tree is dedicated to the survey. The first node offers background information on the survey. The next five nodes allow users to interrogate the database of the survey while the last node shows various statistics and charts as can be seen in the following screenshot.

The interrogation of the database requires that users make four selections. The first is the sentence which they want information on. Then they choose a county or counties from a province which is to be examined in the subsequent operation. A gender specification can be made (or none, the first option) and lastly a value must be chosen which is used in the assessment of survey data. The three options here are the same as those in the PC software for the survey (see discussion above).

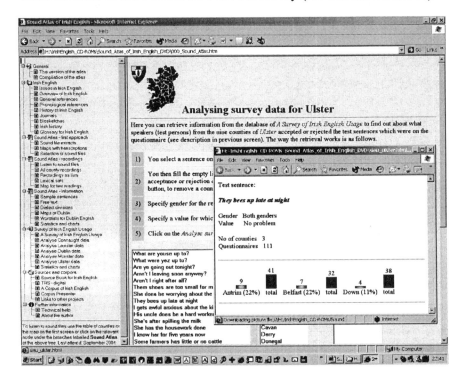

When the necessary information has been provided by selection from the various lists the survey data can be analysed by clicking on the button at the bottom of the screen. A graph is generated and columns can be seen which indicate the relative acceptance of the sentence selected for the analysis.

The graph in the popup window can be copied to the Windows clipboard by simply dragging the mouse over it while holding down the left button. Press Ctrl-C or choose *Copy* from the right button menu when you have selected the entire graph. The graph can now be retrieved into any software, such as your word processor via the *Paste* option or by pressing Ctrl-V.

5. *Tape-Recorded Survey of Hiberno-English Speech – Digital*

The *Tape Recorded Survey of Hiberno-English Speech* is a partially completed survey of English in Ireland. It was initiated in the 1970s by various colleagues at the Department of English, Queen's University, Belfast. The main researcher involved in the planning and coordination was Mr Michael Barry, formerly of this department.

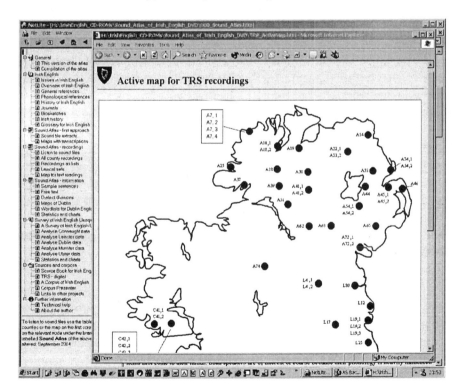

The plan was to cover the entire country by interviewing typical informants from each point in a grid of the island of Ireland (several hundred informants were envisaged for this). Only a fraction of this plan was completed by the time the project came to an untimely close in the early 1980s. A small number of interviewers were involved (both male and female, from the north and south of Ireland, it would appear) who contacted informants and went through a questionnaire with them. After this they recorded some free speech in which they were asked about their locality, their youth, their occupations, etc. The questionnaire consisted of some 374 questions (the text of the questionnaire can be viewed by clicking on the link *Questionnaire used in survey* in the 'TRS' module) in which informants were tested for their pronunciations of key words. These words were not spoken by the interviewer but rather provoked by asking questions in which the relevant key word was the most likely answer. The informants consulted in this survey are generally rural inhabitants and tend to be at least middle-aged, if not older (though there is one young boy on the tapes). Hence the survey is in stark contrast to sociolinguistic investigations done of urban English in Ireland, for instance those by James and Lesley Milroy in Belfast or by the present author in Dublin. Despite these provisos, it is hoped that the survey offers a snapshot of traditional dialects around the island of Ireland in the late 20th century.

The tapes used for the present digitisation were given to the author by Mr Barry in 1984 to whom he is very grateful. The recordings were chosen from the available tapes in order to offer a representative sample of the survey which was then incomplete and which has remained so. The coverage for Ulster is best as here the first informants were found. For the remaining three provinces only a handful of speakers were recorded, but some of these are from Irish-speaking areas which makes the material interesting for research into the syntax of Irish English. In addition, further material from the area of Cork has been included here thanks to Dr Brendan Gunn who kindly put his tapes from this part of Ireland at the author's disposal. The latter's contribution to this project has been to prepare the material for digital processing (digitisation of audio tapes, programming of the Java interface, creation of the active map). The background information has also been supplied by the author who in addition reconstructed the questionnaire text as the original documents have been lost.

V Technical notes

Setup procedure In the root directory of the DVD there is a programme called `setup.exe`. Double-click on this to begin the setup procedure. *A Sound Atlas of Irish English* will be installed on your computer if you go through the various steps which the programme suggests. Bear in mind that you require approximately 3.2 GB (3,200 MB) of free space for both all the sound files and the software contained on the DVD to be installed to the hard disk of your computer. If you choose not to copy the sound files then you only require about 160 MB free space. You can then run the supplied software and listen to the sound files on the DVD which obviously must be inserted into the appropriate drive of your computer.

If you get a message during the setup programme to the effect that a file the programme wishes to copy is available as a newer version on your computer then choose to keep this file. If a so-called 'access violation error' occurs then choose the option *Ignore* in the window which opens at that point.

The setup procedure concludes with the message that the programme has been installed successfully and that a number of links have been created in a desktop folder.

Troubleshooting You should not experience any difficulties with the operation of *A Sound Atlas of Irish English*. However, one or two points must be borne in mind. Assuming that the installation proceeded correctly and that you have ample space on your hard disk, the main prerequisite for the running of the programme is a functioning soundcard.

The files on the present DVD have been compressed to reduce size. The technique used is the original MPEG 'Layer 3' technique (often just called 'MP3') developed by the *Frauenhofer Institut* in Germany. The files all have the extension `.WAV` and can be played automatically by using any version of the Windows *Media Player* supplied with recent versions of Microsoft *Windows*, such as *Windows 2000* or *Windows XP*.

For optimal display of the various maps loaded by the supplied software it is recommended that you choose a screen resolution which is at least 1024 x 768 pixels in size. Anything below this will mean that there is not enough space on the screen to display all information correctly.

Further processing If you wish, you can process the sound files with your own software. For instance, if you are interested in doing spectrographic analysis then you could take any file and import it into appropriate software and analyse the material further. The only request which the author has is that you acknowledge the source of the sound files in any published literature or any material distributed via the internet.

Removing software and data If at some later point you wish to remove *A Sound Atlas of Irish English* then you will have to go through the following three steps: (1) open the *Control Panel* of your computer (via the *Start* button) and select the module *Add/Remove Programs*; remove the current programme from the sets of registered applications in your version of Windows, (2) delete the desktop folder called *A Sound Atlas of Irish English*, (3) go to the folder C:\Program Files by means of the Windows *Explorer* and delete the folder *A Sound Atlas of Irish English* and all subfolders beneath it.

VI Glossary of computer terms

ASCII character set A group of characters which contains 256 symbols available on most personal computers. These include all the letters needed for English and West European languages. Because the characters for other languages such as Chinese, Arabic or Russian and not part of this set, many operating systems now use the *Unicode set which contains many thousand potential characters.

audio adapter, see *soundcard*.

backup Refers to a file which is the last version processed and kept for security purposes; a copy of an original diskette; a procedure for generating such files/copies.

bmp file (= *bitmap*) A graphics file format which is favoured by Windows but which results in files which are unnecessarily large. A much more compact format is found with *JPG files.

browser A programme which enables you to view internet files (in *HTML format, possibly with *JavaScript extensions). This can happen online (via the internet) or offline (when viewing local files on your computer) as with the Java version of *A Sound Atlas of Irish English*.

cancel To terminate a programme, to break off an action. Usually, pressing the Escape key has the function of cancelling whatever operation is pending or currently being carried out.

case sensitive Refers to the fact that upper and lower case letters are *not* treated as the same in the execution of commands or instructions. If a programme has a differing interpretation of alphanumeric data according to whether it is written in capital letters (upper-case) or small letters (lower-case) then it is said to be case-sensitive.

CD-ROM A read-only storage medium consisting of a disc on the surface of which are millions of 'pits' which can be scanned by a laser beam and translated into digital information. CD-ROMs typically have a storage capacity of 650 MB. A *DVD* is similar in form and function to a CD-ROM but can store several gigabyte of data.

clipboard An area of system memory which can be used as a temporary buffer to which data can be written and from which it can be retrieved easily without exiting the programme currently running. You can access data deposited in the Windows clipboard by pressing Ctrl-V or using the Paste option of a programme.

client A term to refer to the computer – and hence the individual – using the internet. See *server*.

cookie A small file which is written to a local computer by a file in the internet. This file can be used to determine, for instance, how often a website has been visited.

corpus Any body of coherent data collected according to criteria laid down in advance. There are many types of corpora of which linguistic corpora are a subset. For the latter a corpus could be a selection of a language variety as is the case with *A Sound Atlas of Irish English* which is an audio corpus. Most linguistic corpora are of written texts, frequently representing diachronic stages or genres of a language.

current directory The directory on disk which is used when loading or saving files, unless you specify another one. Most programmes have the option of determining this by an internal command. The current directory is not normally the directory in which the programme itself is to be found.

customised Created, altered or set-up by the user. A customised version of a programme is thus one which has been tailored by the user to his/her personal needs.

data directory A directory in which data is stored. Normally you move to this directory to process some file(s) in it. The programmes used to process data are not usually kept in the same directory as the data. See *current directory*.

database A file type in which data is arranged in a structure which consists of *fields*, each with a specified name, length and type. The entire database consists of a number of such structures which are termed *records*. In addition the database has a header at the beginning in which information on its structure is contained. This type of organisation facilitates the accurate retrieval of information and the selective extraction of data as with the data of *A Survey of Irish English Usage*.

data set A small text file, with the extension `.dts`, used by the main Windows programme of *A Sound Atlas of Irish English*, which contains a list of the sound files to be displayed in the tree which appears after choosing a data set from a directory list.

dedicated software Any type of software which is designed for a specific purpose, e.g. the Windows programmes of *A Sound Atlas of Irish English*.

default A general reference to a value or name which is assumed unless another is specified by the user. For instance, the default *data set in *A Sound Atlas of Irish English* is that which shows all the available sound files.

desktop A figurative term used to describe the initial level of the user interface – where one arrives on starting one's computer – and where one can undertake various operations from.

directory A division of the available space on a disk which has a name and usually contains several files which belong together. Directories are arranged hierarchically in tree form (with branches and sub-branches) and can be displayed in this form on a certain programme level or by programmes like the file manager contained in the Windows suite for the sound atlas. In Windows the term 'folder' is often used for 'directory'.

display Refers to the representation of data on the computer screen. The size of the display varies and for *A Sound Atlas of Irish English* should be at least 1024 x 768 (a minimum with most modern computers).

download The action of loading files from a remote computer to a local one, e.g. when working with the internet.

DVD (= *digital versatile disc*) A recent standard for encoding information on disks and which can store much more data than conventional CD-ROMs. DVDs have varying capacities depending on whether both sides of the disc are used and on the density of data recording. The DVD of *A Sound Atlas of Irish English* has a capacity of 4.7 GB, 3.2 GB of which is used by data.

Escape-key A key at the upper left-hand corner of most keyboards. It normally has the function of backing out of a command at the last moment (hence the name). It is also used in a quasi-standard fashion for retracing one level back through a programme to a previous level.

extension The letters after the dot in a file name (normally three). There are typical extensions for file types, .LST for list files, .TXT for text files, etc. Programmes often use characteristic extensions for the files they create, for instance .DOC for Microsoft *Word* files. Other files are independent of programmes but nonetheless have a characteristic extension, for example .HTM for internet files (also found in four letter form as .HTML).

folder See **directory.*

formatting data The data which indicates how a document has been formatted with a particular programme and which is responsible for such matters as page layout and fonts. This data can usually be removed from a text file to yield a text file which can then be read by any other programme without being converted in advance.

front end A term for an interface between the user and some software which processes data in the background. There is both a Windows and a Java front end allowing access to the data of *A Sound Atlas of Irish English.*

gigabyte A unit of measurement, typically referring to the capacity of a hard disk or a **DVD and totalling one billion (one thousand MB) bytes. Abbreviated to GB.

HTML (= *Hypertext Markup Language*) A programming language which specifies how text and graphics are to be displayed. This language has enjoyed a great increase in popularity because it is the standard used for internet files. There are several versions of HTML, expansions such as XML (*extensible markup language*) and the superordinate form SGML (*standard generalised markup language*) from which HTML was derived.

INI-file A small text file which is read by one of the major programmes of the Windows suite for *A Sound Atlas of Irish English* on starting. The values for many parameters of these programmes are gained from such a file and used for the subsequent work session. An initialisation file must match the programme which consults it. If not, the programme will behave erratically. These files should not be edited by users.

internet A widely used communication service for making electronic information available through the lines used by telephone systems. The internet is in principle an open system available to anyone who has access to it via a provider. The connection to the provider is usually via the telephone line to which a local computer is connected.

JavaScript An extension to HTML, deriving from the programming language Java developed by Sun microsystems. It provides additional functionality to internet files. Strictly speaking, Java is a separate programming language, but nowadays the short form 'Java' is used when JavaScript is meant, i.e. extensions to HTML files. Most internet browsers, including those in the Windows and Apple *Macintosh* operating systems can process JavaScript additions to HTML files, many of which are included in the Java version of *A Sound Atlas of Irish English*.

JPG file A graphics file format commonly used as a replacement for *bitmap files as it requires only a fraction of the space for storing the same information.

log on A general term used to specify a certain device as the current one, for example to specify that drive C: is the one you wish to work with. It can also be used in networking to denote a set of files or a transmission line used when one begins a work session.

mp3 file A file with audio data which usually stems from a file in the Windows *Wave* format after this has been compressed to a fraction of its original size. MP3 files can have the extension .WAV or .MP3. All the recordings of *A Sound Atlas of Irish English* are in MP3 format with the extension .WAV.

multimedia Any reference to software or hardware which has the ability to process data in several formats, e.g. sound and video data, and not just the conventional text format.

node A point in a tree. A node can be the beginning of a branch or the end of one (a terminal node). A terminal node is associated with a file which is displayed when the node is clicked. This is way in which the Java version of *A Sound Atlas of Irish English* works.

offline Not connected to a network.

online Connected to a network, i.e. when actively linked to the internet.

operating system A set of programme files which are loaded by the computer on starting and which represent the software part of that information which the computer requires to be able to function in the first place, e.g. to load other programmes, to read and save files, to deal with the keyboard and the screen, etc. Windows is the operating system for PCs (Intel-based computers). The Apple *Macintosh* computer family have a different operating system which is not directly compatible with Windows, though the disks formatted for the latter can usually be read by the former system.

pdf file (= *portable data format*) A format, propagated by the American software firm Adobe for their product *Acrobat,* which is intended to specify in a hardware-independent manner how complex texts are to be encoded so as to be readable on any computer supporting the format.

programme structure The way data is accessed and presented to users on a computer. Data structure is not usually the concern of the user. However, in certain cases, as with *A Sound Atlas of Irish English*, users should be aware of the difference between Windows-based software, which has to be installed on a computer running under this operating system, and Java software which is independent of operating systems and can thus be run on more or less any computer.

provider A term referring to a computer service which provides the link between individual customers and the internet. The provider is the firm or institution which enables you to access the internet and to which you log on when starting an internet session.

root directory The main directory of a disk; the top directory below which all others are arranged. It is displayed in the operating system as a single backslash, \.

RTF A specification for text layout and formatting which has been developed to allow texts to be interchangeable between programmes and environments. RTF is an abbreviation for 'Rich Text Format'.

server A term to refer to the provider of internet services. See **client.*

soundcard An item of hardware in a personal computer which controls the production of sound, e.g. when playing audio files. The soundcard must obviously connect to headphones or external speakers. There are differences in the quality of soundcards but for speech files such as those in the sound atlas, this is irrelevant.

subdirectory On a disk, a directory which is located below the root directory. On hard disks there are usually several subdirectories which are arranged in a hierarchy which is intended to reflect the data which is kept in them.

text editor A type of editor which deliberately makes no provision for formatting data (page layout, character attributes, etc.) as the files you edit with such a programme are not primarily intended for printing.

toggle Any key which inverts a state, i.e. turning something *on* if it was *off* and *off* if it was *on*. Many of the commands in the Windows suite for *A Sound Atlas of Irish English* are toggles.

tree display A manner of display which is generally regarded as intuitively easy to grasp as it shows data in a hierarchy realised by nodes and branches arranged in a descending order.

Unicode A means of encoding characters for processing on personal computers. The *ASCII character set uses just one byte and so can only encode 256 characters. The Unicode set, on the other hand, uses two bytes and can thus encode a much greater number of characters, dealing easily with writing systems not based on the Latin alphabet, such as those for Russian, Arabic, Korean, Chinese, Japanese, etc.

upload The process of transferring data away from a local computer to a server as when one loads the data of a webpage up to a provider.

URL An acronym for *universal resource locator*. This is the technical term for an internet address. Such addresses normally begin with `http://www.` and continue with the details of the location in question. The last element (after the last dot) is a reference to a country, e.g. `.ie` = Ireland, `.uk` = United Kingdom, or a superordinate set of internet addresses, e.g. `.com`, `.org` or `.net`.

user interface A term which refers to the way a programme presents itself to a user, what it looks like on the screen, the commands it puts at his/her disposal, or the level at which he/she can communicate with the programme.

wave file A type of file, with the extension `.WAV`, common in the *Windows* environment. It used for storing audio data, see also **mp3 file*.

website A location in the internet used to display data which stem from one source such as a university, a company or in some cases a single individual. A website is accessed via an address, often with the form *http://www.address.organisation.country.*

world wide web Another term for the internet and encoded in most internet addresses as *www.*

VII Timeline for Irish English

early 14c   *Kildare Poems* A set of 16 poems, probably composed somewhere in the east coast of Ireland, between Dublin and Waterford.

1366   *Statutes of Kilkenny* A group of laws which, among many other things, proscribed the use of Irish by the Anglo-Normans in Ireland and insisted that they use English. In order to be understood, the statutes were written in French. In the event they were quite ineffectual.

1577   Richard Stanyhurst's *Treatise containing a Plaine and Perfect Description of Ireland* appeared in *Holinshed's Chronicles* (1577) is published. It contains the first references to the dialect of Forth and Bargy.

1589   *Captain Thomas Stukeley*, the earliest dramatic piece satirising the use of English by the Irish, appears anonymously.

1735   Jonathan Swift *Dialogue in Hybernian stile between A & B*, a parody of the speech of a rural planter and an urban dweller is written.

1781   Thomas Sheridan *A rhetorical grammar of the English language* is published. A prescriptive work with an appendix suggesting corrections to Irish 'mispronunciations of English'.

1788   Charles Vallancey published a glossary of some 28 pages containing words in the dialect of Forth and Bargy, Co Wexford.

1801   *Castle Rackrent* by Maria Edgeworth, considered the first regional novel in English, is published. Many Irish features are to be found in the speech of the main character Thady Quirk, an old retainer who recounts the story of the Rackrents.

1802   Richard and Maria Edgeworth *Essay on Irish Bulls.*

1807   Jacob Poole published a glossary of words from Forth and Bargy; considerably more comprehensive than that of Vallancey.

1845   John Donovan *Grammar of Irish*, the first modern description of the language, appeared.

1860   David Patterson *The provincialisms of Belfast and the surrounding districts pointed out and corrected...* appeared. This is an important source of features of Belfast in the 19th century.

1867   William Barnes published an edition of Poole's glossary of Forth and Bargy with some introductory notes.

1910   Patrick W. Joyce *English as we speak it in Ireland*. This is the first full length monograph on Irish English. The introductory sections on pronunciation and grammar still have a certain value. The part dealing with vocabulary is of less interest today.

1913   Holger Pedersen *Vergleichende Grammatik der keltischen Sprachen* 'Comparative grammar of the Celtic languages' is published.

1927   James Jeremiah Hogan *The English language in Ireland,* a philological work on the development of Irish English since the Middle Ages, appeared.

1932   Thomas F. O'Rahilly *Irish dialects past and present,* which contains references to English in the south-east of the country, is published.

1946   English translation of Rudolf Thurneysen *A grammar of Old Irish* is published in Dublin.

1964   George Brendan Adams (ed.) *Ulster dialects.*

1977   Diarmuid Ó Muirithe (ed.) *The English language in Ireland.*

1979   Alan J. Bliss *Spoken English in Ireland 1600-1740.*

1980   Lesley Milroy *Language and social networks* (2nd edition 1987).

1981   James Milroy *Regional accents of English: Belfast.*

1981   Michael V. Barry (ed.) *Aspects of English dialects in Ireland, Vol. 1. Papers arising from the Tape-Recorded Survey of Hiberno-English Speech.*

1985   John Harris *Phonological variation and change.*

1985   Dónall Ó Baoill (ed.) *Papers on Irish English.*

1986   John Harris, David Little and David Singleton (eds) *Perspectives on the English language in Ireland. Proceedings of the first symposium on Hiberno-English, Dublin 1985.*

1990   Terence P. Dolan (ed.) *The English of the Irish.*

1996   Alison Henry *Belfast English and Standard English. Dialect variation and parameter setting.*

1997   Jeffrey Kallen (ed.) *Focus on Ireland.*

1997   Hildegard Tristram (ed.) *Celtic Englishes. Proceedings of the Potsdam Colloquium on Celtic Englishes, 28-30 September 1995.*

1997   Bernard Share *Slanguage - a dictionary of Irish slang.*

1998   Terence P. Dolan *A dictionary of Hiberno-English.*

1999   James P. Mallory (ed.) *Language in Ulster.*

1999   Markku Filppula *The grammar of Irish English. Language in Hibernian style.*

2000   Tony Crowley *The politics of language in Ireland, 1366-1922.*

2000   Hildegard Tristram (ed.) *Celtic Englishes II. Proceedings of the Second Potsdam Colloquium on Celtic Englishes.*

2001   John Kirk and Dónall Ó Baoill (eds) *Language links. The languages of Scotland and Ireland.*

2002   Raymond Hickey *A Source Book for Irish English.*

2002   John Kirk and Dónall Ó Baoill (eds) *Travellers and their language.*

2002   Zwickl, Simone. *Language attitudes, ethnic identity and dialect use across the Northern Ireland border.*

2003   Hildegard Tristram (ed.) *Celtic Englishes III. Proceedings of the Third Potsdam Colloquium on Celtic Englishes.*

2003   Revised edition of Bernard Share *Slanguage - a dictionary of Irish slang.*

2003   Raymond Hickey *Corpus Presenter. Software for language analysis.* With a manual with A Corpus of Irish English *as sample data.*

2004   Raymond Hickey (ed.) *Legacies of Colonial English.*

2005   Revised edition of Terence P. Dolan *A dictionary of Hiberno-English.*

VIII Glossary for Irish English

ai-retraction A process whereby the onset of the vowel in PRICE is retracted somewhat in Dublin English. This retraction was typical of the now old-fashioned *'Dublin 4' accent (from the 1980s) and is hence not emulated by the younger generation today (2004). For some speakers the retraction may, however, be present before a voiced consonant, i.e. in the PRIDE *lexical set.

au-fronting A process in which speakers use a front starting point for the diphthong of the MOUTH lexical set. A vowel like [æ] or [ɛ] in this position is found in vernacular varieties of English on the east coast, especially in Dublin. A fronted realisation of the MOUTH vowel has spread among young people in Ireland due to the influence of new pronunciations of Dublin English.

Belfast The capital of Ulster at the estuary of the river Lagan in the north east of the country. It was founded in the 17th century and expanded greatly with the development of such industries as ship-building in the 19th century. Linguistically, it is an amalgam of Ulster Scots and Mid-Ulster English inputs along with independent developments of its own, especially in the last century. It is largely Protestant though certain parts, like west Belfast, have Catholic majorities.

Brogue A term stemming from the Irish word either for 'shoe' or 'a knot in the tongue'. Its actual origin cannot be ascertained anymore. The label has been used indiscriminately in the past four centuries for any strongly local accent of Irish English.

Coastal Crescent A term used by Robert Gregg (see references section) to describe a band running from Co. Down, south-east of Belfast, up to Antrim in the extreme north-east, through Co. Derry and across to the north-east of Donegal (but excluding the city of Derry). This area is that of strongest Scottish settlement and is where Ulster Scots is found in its most original form.

Connaught The western-most of the four provinces of Ireland consisting of five counties.

Connemara An area of flat land immediately west of the city of Galway extending out to the mountains towards the west coast. It contains one of the few remaining Irish-speaking areas.

contact Irish English A term describing varieties of English which are in contact with the Irish language via speakers in the few small remaining enclaves scattered along the western seaboard where Irish is still spoken as a native language in a situation of unbroken historical continuity.

Cork The second largest city in the south of Ireland. It has an easily recognisable accent with distinctive intonational patterns not found in the rest of the country.

'Dart' accent A non-linguistic term which has been used in Dublin to describe the new pronunciation of English there. The reference is to the suburban railway line which travels through many upmarket residential areas where this accent is supposed to occur.

Derry The second largest city in Ulster on the banks of the river Foyle near where it enters the sea. It has always had a special status in west Ulster and in the context of the state of Northern Ireland it is remarkable in having a Catholic majority. The name 'Londonderry' stems from the 17th century when London companies were commissioned with the task of settling English people in the city.

Donegal A large county in the extreme north-west of Ireland. It is geographically and linguistically a part of Ulster although included in the state of Northern Ireland. The county also has a small community of Irish speakers along its north-west coast.

Dublin The capital of the Republic of Ireland and by far and away the largest city in the entire island with nearly one third (slightly over 1 million) people living in its metropolitan area.

Dublin English A cover term for a group of varieties of English in the capital of the Republic of Ireland. English here has a long history going back to the late 12th century. The vernacular varieties in the city have a distinct phonetic profile and non-local inhabitants of the city have in the past 15 years or so avoided this by dissociating themselves from the local pronunciation. The new pronunciation which has developed as a result of this process is spreading rapidly in the south of Ireland and will supplant the current mainstream variety in the next generation.

'Dublin 4' accent. A dated reference to a pronunciation of English which was putatively characteristic of those who lived in the upmarket postal district of Dublin 4 in the 1980s. See *Dart accent.*

East Coast A dialect region in Ireland (including the capital Dublin) which is roughly equivalent to the area of original settlement by the Anglo-Normans and English in the late 12th century. This region shows several features not shared by varieties to the north and west of the country, e.g. the occurrence of unshifted [ʊ] in the STRUT lexical set (Dublin) and the archaic uvular [ʁ] of north Leinster.

Forth and Bargy Two baronies in the extreme south-east of Ireland, in Co. Wexford, where a particularly archaic form of English, from the medieval English settlement there, was spoken up to the beginning of the 19th century. There are no phonetic reflexes of this dialect today, but some of its lexical items still survive in south Wexford rural English.

Gaelic A generic term for the Q-Celtic branch of the Insular Celtic languages consisting of Irish, Scottish Gaelic and Manx. In a Scottish context the bare term 'Gaelic' or 'Gallick' (reflecting the local pronunciation) is taken to refer to Scottish Gaelic.

Gaeltacht An Irish term meaning 'Irish-speaking area'. There are two types of Irish-speaking area which have been given official status, Fíor-Gaeltacht, the true Gaeltacht with a high density of Irish speakers, and Breach-Gaeltacht, those areas in which the number of native speakers in considerably less.

Hibernia The Latin word for Ireland, possibly deriving from the word for 'winter' but more likely from the name of an ancient tribe associated with Ireland.

Irish The name for either the people of Ireland or the Celtic language still spoken by a small minority chiefly on the western seaboard.

Leinster One of the four provinces of Ireland in the east, south-east of the island, consisting of 12 counties.

lexical set A reference to a group of words all of which have the same pronunciation for a certain sound. For instance, the lexical set TRAP is used to refer to the pronunciation which speakers of a variety have for the sound which is /æ/ in RP.

linguistic area A term used to describe a geographically delimited area in which languages and/or varieties share structural properties and features which are independent of any possible genetic relationship.

***l*-velarisation** A process whereby laterals are pronounced with the lowering of the body and the raising of the back of the tongue yielding a characteristic hollow sound. This is typical of new pronunciations of Dublin English.

Midlands The centre of Ireland which is a flat expanse bordered by the hills and mountains which occupy the coastal regions of the country. This expanse stretches from an area west of Co. Dublin as far as the Shannon linking up with east Clare, Galway and Mayo and on a north-south axis delimited by the border with Northern Ireland in the north and to the south by a line running roughly from Limerick across to Dublin.

Mid Ulster English A term referring to that section of the population of Ulster which is derived from English settlers of the 17th century and is one of the two major linguistic groupings in Northern Ireland, the other being Ulster Scots. Also referred to as *Ulster Anglo-Irish.*

Munster One of the four provinces of Ireland in the south, south-west of the island, consisting of six counties.

nasal raising A process whereby vowels are articulated from a slightly raised position when immediately preceding nasal sounds. The vowel affected by this in the south west and lower west of Ireland is /ɛ/ which is pronounced as /ɪ/ leading to the so-called PEN/PIN merger.

Northern Ireland Since 1921 a state within the United Kingdom. It consists of six of the nine counties of the province of Ulster and was created as an option for the Protestant majority in the north-east of Ireland, descended from original Scottish and English settlers, to remain within the British union.

Old English A reference to the English settlers in pre-Reformation Ireland, i.e. to the descendants of the late medieval settlers who came at the end of the 12th century. This group was mostly assimilated to the native Irish, especially outside the *Pale.

Pale A term for the area of Dublin, its immediate hinterland and a stretch of the east coast down to the south-east corner which was fairly successful in resisting increasing Gaelicisation up to the 16th century. The varieties of English in this area still show features which stem from late medieval Irish English whereas those further west in the country show greater evidence of influence from Irish, the native language before the switch-over to English.

Republic of Ireland Since 1949 the official name for the south of Ireland (excluding *Northern Ireland). With the declaration of a republic, Ireland left the Commonwealth and formally achieved a greater degree of independence from the United Kingdom.

retentionist view A standpoint in Irish English studies where considerable weight is accorded to regional English input to Ireland in the genesis of the specific forms of English there. This stance implies that the Irish language is not assumed to have played a central role. See *substratist view*.

rhoticity A reference to the degree to which vowels are pronounced with r-colouring (realised by curling back the tip of the tongue). Local Dublin English is only slightly rhotic, i.e. has low rhoticity.

r-**retroflexion** A process whereby vowels are pronounced with the tip of the tongue curled back noticeably towards the hard palate, thus evincing high rhoticity. This is in contrast and probably a reaction to the situation in local Dublin English.

Scouse The city dialect of Liverpool which, due to heavy Irish immigration to the Merseyside region in the 19th century, shows not insignificant traces of Irish English, for example in the lenition of stops.

Shelta The assumed language of the Irish travelling people of which only a little is known (vocabulary and some grammatical features). The language is scarcely accessible today and not assumed to be the robust native speech of travelling people, even if this was in fact once the case.

sibilant fortition A feature of south-east vernacular Irish English where /z/ is pronounced as /d/ in function words when followed by another consonant, e.g. *isn't* ['ɪdn̩t].

'slit' *t* A reference to the pronunciation of /t/ as an apico-alveolar fricative in weak positions (intervocalically or word-finally after a vowel and before a pause). This articulation shares all features with the stop /t/ but is a continuant. The realisation is ubiquitous in the south of Ireland and common in the north as well. It is also found, as a transferred feature, in the speech of the Irish-derived community in Newfoundland.

SOFT-lengthening A process which is typical of east coast urban Irish English, above all of Dublin English, where the vowel in words of the SOFT lexical set, e.g. *off, cross,* etc., are pronounced with a long vowel.

South-West An area in the south-west of Ireland, which consists primarily of the two large counties Cork and Kerry, and which has a number of distinct features, such as *nasal raising and distinctive intonational patterns.

substratist view A standpoint in Irish English studies where considerable weight is accorded to structural transfer from Irish into English during the genesis of the specific forms of English in Ireland. This stance implies that regional English input is not assumed to have played a central role. See *retentionist view.*

supraregionalisation A process in which salient vernacular features of a variety are replaced by more standard ones, frequently from an extranational norm, as with southern British English vis à vis Irish English. The motivation for this move is to render a variety less locally bound and thus more acceptable to the non-vernacular community.

transition area A reference to an area stretching from Co. Sligo in the north-west to Co. Louth in north Leinster and which shares features of both the north and the south of Ireland.

***u*-fronting** A term to refer to the pronunciation of items from the GOOSE lexical set with a high mid vowel. This pronunciation also applies to diphthongs which contain /u/, i.e. to that in the MOUTH lexical set. This is an areal feature which Ulster shares with Scotland.

Ullans A term for Ulster Scots which has been formed on analogy with Lallans, the indigenous label for Lowland Scots.

Ulster Scots The language of the Scottish settlers, in the coastal regions in the north and north-east of Ulster, and of their descendants. Much assimilation and mixing have taken place in the past few centuries especially in cities like Belfast.

Ulster A province of Ireland in the north of the country. It consists of nine counties, six of which now form the state of Northern Ireland. Co Donegal in the extreme north-west is part of the Republic of Ireland but has more linguistic features in common with speech in Northern Ireland, both with Ulster Scots and Mid-Ulster English.

universalist view A kind of 'third way' in Irish English studies which is seen as complementing both the *substratist and *retentionist views. In essence it assumes that there are universals of uncontrolled adult second language acquisition which are similar in many ways to those operative in creolisation, but not identical of course. These are assumed to be responsible for many specific structures, such as verbal aspect distinctions, which arose during the language switch-over from Irish to English.

vernacularisation A process in which non-local speakers style-shift downwards to achieve a vernacular effect. An example of this would be the use of *youse* or *yez* for the second person plural in Ireland. This is normally avoided by non-local speakers but can be employed when deliberately switching to a vernacular mode.

West A reference to the large area of western Ireland from Clare up to Sligo. Of all areas of the country this was Irish-speaking longest.

word list style A type of reading style in which informants read single words from a list. Speakers tend to be least vernacular in their speech when reading such lists.

Yola The form of the word 'old' in the dialect of Forth and Bargy which came to be used as a reference to the dialect itself.

References

Adams, George Brendan
    1958   The emergence of Ulster as a distinct dialect area, *Ulster Folklife* 4, 61-73.
    1965   Materials for a language map of 17th century Ireland, *Ulster Dialect Archive Bulletin* 4: 15-30.

Adams, George Brendan (ed.)
    1964   *Ulster dialects: An introductory symposium.* Holywood, Co. Down: Ulster Folk and Transport Museum.

Algeo, John (ed.)
    2001   *English in North America. Cambridge History of the English Language*, Vol. 6. Cambridge: University Press.

Bailey, Richard W. and Manfred Görlach (eds.)
    1982   *English as a world language.* Ann Arbor: University of Michigan Press.

Barry, Michael V.
    1981   The southern boundaries of northern Hiberno-English speech, in Barry (ed.), 52-95.

Barry, Michael (ed.)
    1981   *Aspects of English dialects in Ireland, Vol 1. Papers arising from the Tape-Recorded Survey of Hiberno-English Speech.* Belfast: Institute for Irish Studies.

Beal, Joan
    1993   The grammar of Tyneside and Northumbrian English, in Milroy and Milroy (eds.), 187-213.

Bhaldraithe, Tomás de
    1945   *The Irish of Cois Fhairrge, Co. Galway.* Dublin: Institute for Advanced Studies.

Bliss, Alan J.
    1972   Languages in contact. Some problems of Hiberno-English, *Proceeding of the Royal Irish Academy*, Section C, 72, 63-82.
    1976   The English language in early modern Ireland, in Moody, Martin and Byrne (eds.), 546-60.
    1977   The emergence of modern English dialects in Ireland, in Ó Muirithe (ed.), 7-19.
    1979   *Spoken English in Ireland 1600-1740. Twenty-seven representative texts assembled and analysed.* Dublin: Cadenus Press.
    1984   English in the south of Ireland, in Trudgill (ed.), 135-51.

Brinton, Laurel (ed.)
    2001   *Historical linguistics 1999.* Amsterdam: John Benjamins.

Burchfield, Robert (ed.)
1994   *English in Britain and overseas: Origins and development. The Cambridge History of the English Language.* Vol. 5. Cambridge: University Press.
Clarke, Sandra
1997   The role of Irish English in the formation of New World Englishes. The case from Newfoundland, in Kallen (ed.), 207-25.
Clarke, Sandra (ed.)
1993   *Focus on Canada.* Varieties of English around the World, General Series, Vol. 11. Amsterdam: John Benjamins.
Corrigan, Karen P.
1997   The acquisition and properties of a contact vernacular grammar, in Anders Ahlqvist and Vera Čapková (eds.) 1997. *Dán do oide. Essay in memory of Conn R. Ó Cléirigh.* Dublin: Linguistics Institute of Ireland, 75-93.
1999   Language contact and language shift in County Armagh 1178-1659, in Mallory (ed.), 54-69.
Dolan, Terence P.
2005 [1998]   *A dictionary of Hiberno-English. The Irish use of English.* Dublin: Gill and Macmillan.
Dolan, Terence P. (ed.)
1990   *The English of the Irish. Irish University Review, 20:1* Dublin: n.p.
Dudley Edwards, Ruth
1981 [1973]   *An atlas of Irish history.* London: Methuen.
Filppula, Markku
1993   Changing paradigms in the study of Hiberno-English, *Irish University Review* 23:2, 202-23.
1999   *The grammar of Irish English. Language in Hibernian style.* London: Routledge.
2004   The morphology and syntax of Irish-English, in Kortmann et al. (eds.).
Fisiak, Jacek (ed.)
1995   *Language change under contact conditions.* Berlin: Mouton de Gruyter.
Foulkes, Paul and Gerry Docherty (eds.)
1999   *Urban voices.* London: Edward Arnold.
Fry, Dennis
1979   *The physics of speech.* Cambridge: University Press.
Greene, David
1979   Perfects and perfectives in modern Irish, *Ériu* 30, 122-41.
Gregg, Robert J.
1964   Scotch-Irish urban speech in Ulster, in Adams (ed.), 163-92.
1972   The Scotch-Irish dialect boundaries in Ulster, in Wakelin (ed.), 109-39.

1985   *The Scotch-Irish dialect boundary in the province of Ulster.*
            Ottawa: Canadian Federation for the Humanities.
Grundy, Peter
1995   *Doing pragmatics.* London: Edward Arnold.
Harris, John
1983   The Hiberno-English 'I've it eaten' construction: What is it and
            where does it come from?, *Teanga* 3, 30-43.
1984   Syntactic variation and dialect divergence, *Journal of Linguistics*
            20, 303-27.
1986   Expanding the superstrate: habitual aspect markers in Atlantic
            Englishes, *English World-Wide* 7, 171-99.
1993   The grammar of Irish English, in Milroy and Milroy (eds.), 139-
            86.
Henry, Alison
1997   The syntax of Belfast English in Kallen (ed.), 89-108.
Henry, Patrick Leo
1958   A linguistic survey of Ireland. Preliminary report, *Norsk Tidsskrift
            for Sprogvidenskap [Lochlann, A Review of Celtic Studies]*
            Supplement 5, 49-208.
Heuser, Wilhelm
1904   *Die Kildare-Gedichte. Die ältesten mittelenglischen Denkmäler in
            anglo-irischer Überlieferung.* Bonner Beiträge zur Anglistik, Vol.
            14. Bonn: Hanstein.
Hickey, Raymond
1984   Coronal segments in Irish English, *Journal of Linguistics* 20, 233-
            51.
1986a   Possible phonological parallels between Irish and Irish English,
            English World-Wide 7, 1-21.
1986b   Issues in the vowel phoneme inventory of Cois Fhairrge Irish,
            Éigse 31, 214-26.
1988   A lost Middle English dialect: the case of Forth and Bargy, in
            Fisiak (ed.), 235-72.
1993   The beginnings of Irish English, *Folia Linguistica Historica* 14,
            213-38.
1995   An assessment of language contact in the development of Irish
            English, in Fisiak (ed.), 109-30.
1997   Arguments for creolisation in Irish English, in Hickey and Puppel
            (eds.), 969-1038.
1999a   Ireland as a linguistic area, in Mallory (ed.), 36-53.
1999b   Dublin English: Current changes and their motivation, in Foulkes
            and Docherty (eds.), 265-81.
2000a   Dissociation as a form of language change, *European Journal of
            English Studies* 4:3, 303-15.
2000b   Salience, stigma and standard, in Wright (ed.), 57-72.
2001   The South-East of Ireland. A neglected region of dialect study, in
            Kirk and Ó Baoill (eds.), 1-22.

2002   *A source book for Irish English* Amsterdam: John Benjamins.
2003a   *Corpus Presenter. Software for language analysis. With a manual
          and* A Corpus of Irish English *as sample data.* Amsterdam: John
          Benjamins.
2003b   What's cool in Irish English? Linguistic change in contemporary
          Ireland, in Tristram (ed.), pp. 357-73.
2003c   How and why supraregional varieties arise, in Marina Dossena and
          Charles Jones (eds) *Insights into Late Modern English.* Frankfurt:
          Peter Lang, pp. 351-73.
2003d   Rectifying a standard deficiency. Pronominal distinctions in
          varieties of English, in Irma Taavitsainen and Andreas H. Jucker
          (eds), *Diachronic perspectives on address term systems,*
          Pragmatics and Beyond, New Series, Vol. 107. Amsterdam:
          Benjamins, 345–74.
2004   The phonology of Irish English, in Schneider et al. (eds.).
2005   Standard wisdoms and historical dialectology: the discrete use of
          historical regional corpora, in Marina Dossena (ed.) *Proceedings
          of the First International Conference on English Historical
          Dialectology, Bergamo, Italy, 4-6 September 2003.* Frankfurt:
          Lang.

Hickey, Raymond and Stanisław Puppel (eds.)
    1997   *Language History and Linguistic Modelling. A Festschrift for
              Jacek Fisiak on his 60th Birthday.* Berlin: Mouton de Gruyter.

Hindley, Reg
    1990   *The death of the Irish language. A qualified obituary.* London:
              Routledge.

Hogan, James Jeremiah
    1927   *The English language in Ireland.* Dublin: Educational Company of
              Ireland.

Johnson, Barbara
    2000   *Qualitative methods in sociolinguistics.* Oxford: University Press.

Jones, Charles (ed.)
    1997   *The Edinburgh history of the Scots language.* Edinburgh:
              University Press.

Kallen, Jeffrey L.
    1994   English in Ireland, in Burchfield (ed.), 148-96.

Kallen, Jeffrey L. (ed.)
    1997   *Focus on Ireland.* Amsterdam: John Benjamins.

Kirk, John and Dónall Ó Baoill (eds.)
    2001   *Language links: the languages of Scotland and Ireland.* Belfast
              Studies in Language, Culture and Politics, 2. Belfast: Queen's
              University.

Kirkwood, Harry (ed.)
    1986   *Studies in intonation.* Occasional Papers in Linguistics and
              Language Learning. Coleraine: New University of Ulster.

Kirwin, William J.
  1993   The planting of Anglo-Irish in Newfoundland, in Clarke (ed.), 65-84.
Klemola, Juhani
  2000   The origins of the Northern Subject Rule: A case of early contact?, in Tristram (ed.), 329-46.
Kortmann, Bernd, Kate Burridge, Rajend Mesthrie, Edgar Schneider and Clive Upton (eds.)
  2004   *A handbook of varieties of English. A multimedia reference tool.* Vol. 2: Morphology and Syntax. Berlin and New York: Mouton de Gruyter.
Labov, William
  1966   *The social stratification of English in New York City.* Washington, DC: Center for Applied Linguistics.
Lass, Roger
  1990   Early mainland residues in Southern Hiberno-English, in Dolan (ed.), 137-48.
Lucas, Angela (ed.)
  1995   *Anglo-Irish poems of the Middle Ages.* Dublin: Columba Press.
Mallory, James P. (ed.)
  1999   *Language in Ulster.* Special issue of *Ulster Folklife* (45).
McCafferty, Kevin
  1999   (London)Derry: Between Ulster and local speech – class, ethnicity and language change, in Foulkes and Docherty (eds.), 246-64.
  2001   *Ethnicity and language change. English in (London)Derry, Northern Ireland.* Amsterdam: John Benjamins.
McElholm, Dermot D.
  1986   Intonation in Derry English, in Kirkwood (ed.), 1-58.
Milroy, James
  1981   *Regional accents of English: Belfast.* Belfast: Blackstaff.
Milroy, James and Lesley Milroy (eds.)
  1993   *Real English. The grammar of the English dialects in the British Isles.* Real Language Series. London: Longman.
Mitchell, Frank
  1976   *The Irish landscape.* London: Collins.
Montgomery, Michael
  2001   British and Irish antecedents, in Algeo (ed.), 86-153.
Montgomery, Michael and Robert Gregg
  1997   The Scots language in Ulster, in Jones (ed.), 569-622.
Moody, Theodore W., Francis X. Martin and F. J. Byrne (eds.)
  1976   *A new history of Ireland.* Vol. III: Early modern Ireland (1534-1691). Oxford: Clarendon Press.
Ní Chasaide, Ailbhe
  1979   Laterals in Gaoth-Dobhair Irish and Hiberno-English, in Ó Baoill (ed.), 54-78.

Ó Baoill, Dónall
    1991   Contact phenomena in the phonology of Irish and English in Ireland, in Ureland and Broderick (eds.), 581-95.
Ó Baoill, Dónall (ed.)
    1979   *Papers in Celtic phonology.* Coleraine: New University of Ulster.
Ó Cuív, Brian (ed.)
    1969   *A view of the Irish language.* Dublin: Stationary Office.
Ó Muirithe, Diarmuid
    1996   *Dictionary of Anglo-Irish. Words and phrases from Irish.* Dublin: Four Courts Press.
Ó Muirithe, Diarmuid (ed.)
    1977   *The English language in Ireland.* Cork: Mercier.
Ó Sé, Diarmuid
    1992   The perfect in Modern Irish, *Ériu* 43, 39-67.
Rahilly, Joan
    1997   Aspects of prosody in Hiberno-English: The case of Belfast, in Kallen (ed.), 109-32.
Schneider, Edgar, Kate Burridge, Bernd Kortmann, Rajend Mesthrie and Clive Upton (eds.)
    2004   *A handbook of varieties of English. A multimedia reference tool.* Vol. 1: Phonology. Berlin and New York: Mouton de Gruyter.
Sheridan, Thomas
    1781   *A rhetorical grammar of the English language calculated*
    1782   *solely for the purpose of teaching propriety of pronunciation and justness of delivery, in that tongue.* Dublin: Price.
Stenson, Nancy
    1991   Code-switching vs. borrowing in Modern Irish, in Ureland and Broderick (eds.), 559-79.
Stubbs, Michael
    1983   *Discourse analysis. The sociolinguistic analysis of natural language.* Oxford: Blackwell.
Sullivan, James P.
    1976   *The genesis of Hiberno-English: A socio-historical account.* PhD thesis. New York: Yeshiva University.
    1980   The validity of literary dialect: evidence from the theatrical portrayal of Hiberno-English, *Language and Society* 9, 195-219.
Thomason, Sarah G. and Terence Kaufman
    1988   *Language contact, creolization, and genetic linguistics.* Berkeley, Los Angeles, London: University of California Press.
Tristram, Hildegard L.C. (ed.)
    2000   *The Celtic Englishes II.* Heidelberg: Carl Winter.
    2003   *The Celtic Englishes III.* Heidelberg: Carl Winter.
Trudgill, Peter (ed.)
    1984   *Language in the British Isles.* Cambridge: University Press.

Ureland, P. Sture and George Broderick (eds.)
    1991   *Language contact in the British Isles. Proceedings of the Eighth International Symposium on Language Contact in Europe.* Tübingen: Niemeyer.

Vennemann gen. Nierfeld, Theo
    2000   English as a 'Celtic' language, in Tristram (ed.), 399-406.
    2001   Atlantis Semitica. Structural contact features in Celtic and English, in Brinton (ed.), 351-69.

Wagner, Heinrich
    1959   *Das Verbum in den Sprachen der britischen Inseln.* Tübingen: Niemeyer.

Wakelin, Martyn (ed.)
    1972   *Patterns in the folk speech of the British Isles.* London: Athlone Press.

Wells, John C.
    1982   *Accents of English.* 3 Vols. Cambridge: University Press.

Wright, Laura (ed.)
    2000   *The development of standard English 1300-1800. Theories, descriptions, conflicts.* Cambridge: University Press.

Index

Topics in English Linguistics

Edited by Bernd Kortmann and
Elizabeth Closs Traugott

Mouton de Gruyter · Berlin · New York

20 Christiane Dalton-Puffer, *The French Influence on Middle English Morphology. A Corpus-Based Study on Derivation.* 1996.

21 Johan Elsness, *The Perfect and the Preterite in Contemporary and Earlier English.* 1997.

22 Carl Bache and Niels Davidsen-Nielsen, *Mastering English. An Advanced Grammar for Non-native and Native Speakers.* 1997.

23 *English in Transition. Corpus-based Studies in Linguistic Variation and Genre Styles.* Edited by Matti Rissanen, Merja Kytö and Kirsi Heikkonen. 1997.

24 *Grammaticalization at Work. Studies of Long-term Developments in English.* Edited by Matti Rissanen, Merja Kytö and Kirsi Heikkonen. 1997.

25 Axel Hübler, *The Expressivity of Grammar. Grammatical Devices Expressing Emotion across Time.* 1998.

26 *Negation in the History of English.* Edited by Ingrid Tieken-Boon van Ostade, Gunnel Tottie and Wim van der Wurff. 1998.

27 Martina Häcker, *Adverbial Clauses in Scots: A Semantic-Syntactic Study.* 1998.

28 Ingo Plag, *Morphological Productivity. Structural Constraints in English Derivation.* 1999.

29 Gustav Muthmann, *Reverse English Dictionary. Based on Phonological and Morphological Principles.* 1999.

30 *Metaphor and Metonymy at the Crossroads. A Cognitive Perspective.* Edited by Antonio Barcelona. 2000.

31 *Generative Theory and Corpus Studies. A Dialogue from 10 ICEHL.* Edited by Ricardo Bermúdez-Otero, David Denison, Richard M. Hogg and C. B. McCully. 2000.

32 Manfred G. Krug, *Emerging English Modals. A Corpus-Based Study of Grammaticalization.* 2000.

33 *Cause – Condition – Concession – Contrast. Cognitive and Discourse Perspectives.* Edited by Elizabeth Couper-Kuhlen and Bernd Kortmann. 2000.

34 Hans-Jörg Schmid, *English Abstract Nouns as Conceptual Shells. From Corpus to Cognition.* 2000.

35 *Placing Middle English in Context.* Edited by Irma Taavitsainen, Terttu Nevalainen, Päivi Pahta and Matti Rissanen. 2000.

36 Michael G. Getty, *The Metre of* Beowulf. *A Constraint-based Approach* 2002.

37 Renaat Declerck and Susan Reed, *Conditionals. A Comprehensive Empirical Analysis.* 2001.

38 Alexander Kautzsch, *The Historical Evolution of Earlier African American English. An Empirical Comparison of Early Sources.* 2002.

39 *Studies in the History of the English Language. A Millennial Perspective.* Edited by Donka Minkova and Robert Stockwell. 2002.

40 *A Valency Dictionary of English.* Edited by Thomas Herbst, David Heath, Ian Roe and Dieter Götz. Forthcoming.

42 Anette Rosenbach, *Genitive Variation in English. Conceptual Factors in Synchronic and Diachronic Studies.* 2002.

43 *Determinants of Grammatical Variation in English.* Edited by Günter Rohdenburg and Britta Mondorf. 2003.

44 *Modality in Contemporary English.* Edited by Roberta Facchinetti, Manfred Krug and Frank Palmer. 2003.

45 *Studies in the History of the English Language II: Unfolding Conversations.* Edited by Anne Curzan and Kimberly Emmons. 2004.

47 Ute Dons, *Descriptive Adequacy of Early Modern English Grammars.* 2004.